THE HOW OF SPIRITUAL GROWTH

North Carolina Wesleyan College Library

Scurry - Drum Collection

Given by:
Dr. Frank Scurry and
Carolina Evangelical
Divinity School

THE HOW OF SPIRITUAL GROWTH

by

Robert L. McDonald, MD

A psychiatrist shows how spiritual growth equals psychological change.

Previous works by the author:

God Can Renew Your Mind Through Memory Healing

NC WESLEYAN COLLEGE LIBRARY
ROCKY MOUNT, NC 27804

BRIDGE PUBLISHING, INC.
Publishers of:
LOGOS • HAVEN • OPEN SCROLL

*Unless otherwise noted,
all Scripture quotations in this book
are from the King James Version of the Bible.*

The How of Spiritual Growth
Copyright © 1983 by Bridge Publishing, Inc.
All Rights Reserved
Printed in the United States of America
Library of Congress Catalog Card Number: 83-71168
International Standard Book Number: 0-88270-546-6
Bridge Publishing, Inc., South Plainfield, NJ 07080

My heartfelt gratitude is expressed to two people who have been particularly helpful in the preparation of this manuscript. To my wife, Rita, who was invaluable as a sounding board and critic of ideas throughout the work.

To Evelyn Campbell, whose editing I very much admire; her skill converted my sometimes ponderous and convoluted writing style to phrases which are eminently readable.

Contents

Foreword	xi
Preface	xv
Introduction—"Growth"	xvii
1. What and Where Is Your Spirit?	1
2. In Wisdom and Stature Physical and Psychological Growth	14
3. And in Favor With God and Man Parellels in Spiritual and Personality Growth	24
4. But That's Just the Way I Was Born! A Backward Glance	36
5. What's Personality?	51
6. The Why of Personality Its Determinants	73
7. The Windows of the Mind How Mind Affects Personality	92
8. Why Do I Do That? Motivators of Behavior	115
9. How We Grow Spiritually Spiritual Growth: Its Means	141
10. Why and Where We Grow Spiritual Growth: Its Explanation	154
11. How to Help Yourself Grow The Believer's Response	199
12. Others Can Help You Grow Human Support Systems	222

Dedication

In His timely way God has graciously placed various people in my path. Foremost among them are three men whose lives total 125 years of dedicated Christian service. They have been living models for those whose lives they have touched, including mine.

These three men—Dr. M.G. McLuhan, Dr. Paul L. Walker, and Rev. J.F. Wooderson, all pastors at Mt. Paran Church of God in Atlanta—have the commonality of godliness but diverse administrative roles.

As an academician and linguistic scholar, Dr. McLuhan ranks among Pentecostals as one of the most renowned Bible teachers. His depth of learning has been invaluable in his work as associate pastor. Through his teaching one can begin to see the depth of God's unlimited mind.

Dr. Paul Walker stands in the midst of the three. His daily sacrifices for his flock and his constant compassion truly mark him as having a shepherd's heart. His preaching of the Word is consistently anointed, allowing a freedom of worship not often seen. Paul Walker is my shepherd, my friend, my professional colleague and my inspiration.

The Rev. J.F. Wooderson has accomplished, as part of his lifelong service to God, the remarkable feat of pastoring the Durban, South Africa, Church of God for forty consecutive years! Once retired, Rev. Wooderson was recalled by the Holy Spirit as minister of visitation at Mt. Paran. Leavened by a half-century of Christian service, his Sunday school teaching, coupled with his vibrant white hair and radiantly joyful countenance, reveals that he is a chosen child of God.

Many people have thanked God privately over the years for these men's lives and have wished to thank them in a public manner. Joining with these believers in this desire, I affectionately dedicate this book to these three beloved men.

Foreword

After He had revealed the power of God by healing the multitudes who came to Him, the Lord Jesus gave His disciples the power to proclaim the gospel and heal the sick (Luke 9:1, TEV). The biblical account of His healings of the physical body are dramatic demonstrations of this power, but it is the healing of the diseases of the soul and the spirit that produce the remarkable changes in behavior observed in His followers. These changes have attracted the attention of the world.

Christians came into the Kingdom of God because they believed the Gospel, but they also listened to the teachings of the Apostle Paul, who tells them that "people who are immoral, or who worship idols, or are adulterers, or homosexual perverts, or who steal, or are greedy, or are drunkards, or who slander others, or are thieves—none of these will possess God's Kingdom." Then Paul notes, "Some of you were like that. But you have been purified from sin; you have been dedicated to God; you have been put right with God by the Lord Jesus Christ and by the Spirit of our God" (1 Cor. 6:9-11, TEV). Is it not a tragedy that modern Christianity has ignored the message of sanctification and traded it for the beliefs of secular systems that can only help man to see his depravity but can do nothing about it?

Robert McDonald has written this book on wholeness to reemphasize to the Church the healing power that is available as a result of faith in Jesus Christ. He recognizes that all truth is God's and comes from Him, so he has attempted to utilize the truths he has learned during his psychiatric career to supplement scriptural truth. The latter is used as the foundation on which Dr. McDonald builds his system of spiritual growth and psychological change. He emphatically brings to our attention the initial work of the Holy Spirit in bringing about change. Dr. McDonald does not, however, overemphasize this work for, like all of us engaged in this work, he has observed that there is a need for further growth after one receives the Holy Spirit at salvation. His book emphasizes the need for teaching and counseling as the means by which persons who come into the Christian life are made clean (John 15:3) and bear the fruit that our Lord desired.

To guide persons who need counseling and those who seek to counsel, he has discussed the nature of man and how this nature, in conjunction with the roles of parents, siblings, and culture, influences the development of personality. Dr. McDonald neither overemphasizes nor minimizes the importance of man's sinful nature in creating the problems so often observed. He appropriately recognizes the roles of salvation in dealing with this nature, but he is also cognizant of the necessity for continuing one's salvation (Phil. 2:12) through discipleship. He considers discipleship to be the development of the disciplines of prayer, Bible study and worship. In addition, he describes the necessity of counseling, memory healing, self-image enhancement, and the management of forces and drives. Dr. McDonald believes also that the support community of the Church is necessary to provide encouragement and acceptance in order that the growing Christian may be appropriately nurtured in the faith.

The content of this book is not "pop psychology" with a theological theme, or theology with a simplistic psychological theme, but it is instead an in-depth look at the origins of the need for growth and the direction in which a person must be moved to accomplish it.

As I read the manuscript, I frequently found myself nodding in agreement as the author lucidly presented one insight after another. The Kingdom of God will be blessed by this book, for Dr. McDonald has not tried to impress us with his knowledge by using big words or great learning (1 Cor. 2:1-5), but he has presented the inherent healing power of the Lord's message in easy-to-read language that is readily understood. I appreciated this, for it is evidence of a humility that glorifies the Lord. Dr. Robert McDonald has indeed shown that "the supreme power belongs to God and not to us."

—William P. Wilson, MD
Professor, Department of Psychiatry
Duke University Medical School
Durham, North Carolina

Preface

It has been aptly said that while "salvation is God's gift to the sinner, discipleship is the saint's gift to God." Being a disciple brings the saint into fruitfulness in his new life. Since discipleship implies spiritual growth, this process is, or should be, of utmost importance to any believer who is walking the route of discipleship.

The purpose of this book is to show how spiritual growth relates to psychological background and change. While our focus will be both divine and human, we will spotlight the psychological dimensions. Spiritual growth is not a disembodied process. As a spiritual being, man lives within the confines of his mind, bounded by its limitations and anchored to the past through its workings. The disciple can, I believe, aid his own spiritual growth if he understands his psychological makeup, the interrelationships of its various parts and the process by which these are gradually transformed.

For too long this transformation has been fraught with vagueness, extending at times to mystical overtones. Lack of understanding has stymied many believers in their pursuit of spiritual growth. They experience a sense of helplessness. Or they engage in puzzled attempts to 'make it happen.'

Regarding the latter, I am reminded of how a caged animal, trying to get out, may accidentally trip the release and free itself. However, when it is put back in the cage the animal can make only random sequences of movements because it does not know the key to release. Eventually it may trip it again. But how uneconomical of time and effort, not only in promoting release, but also in gaining understanding which can be generalized to other 'tight spots.'

Certainly I am not suggesting that believers are caged animals. Indeed, they are truly free humans—free by virtue of possessing an essential relationship with God, the Father, the Divine Creator. Our question is how to enhance the relationship, how to nurture and sponsor its growth so that the fruitfulness therein can develop more of the potential God created in each believer.

My hope is that this work will provide some answers. *Some* answers because, despite the advancing state of our knowledge, "we know in part, and we prophesy in part" (1 Cor. 13:9). Yet, even partial answers can decrease fruitless groping and can guide the believer more surely along the path of spiritual growth.

This book was initiated at the direction of the Holy Spirit. Its chapter-by-chapter progression saw a change in direction from the initial outline to its present form. The hours of labor involved in bringing this book to birth necessitated 'redoing some of my first works.' Time-worn concepts that were longtime friends had to be reexamined like last year's clothing. Some were discarded as being out of date. Some were found to be eminently serviceable. And some new ones were included. My thinking became more incisive, and my perspective sharpened. As a result I have a greater appreciation for God's handiwork.

In the process of writing I became a more effective therapist. May the Chief Author minister to members of His Body, the collective believers in Christ, through reading this work, just as He ministered to me in its writing.

Introduction—"Growth"

When I consider thy heavens, the work of thy fingers, the moon and the stars, which thou hast ordained;
What is man, that thou art mindful of him? and the son of man, that thou visitest him?
For thou hat made him a little lower than the angels, and hast crowned him with glory and honour.
Thou madest him to have dominion over the works of thy hands; thou hast put all things under his feet. (Ps. 8:3-6)

The whole of God's creation heralds constant change. At times this change is orchestrated in a muted way, as in the almost imperceptible, progressive opening of a rose bud to velvety, showy perfection. At other times change is more dramatic, violent, strident, as demonstrated by the sudden awakening of the long-dormant Mount St. Helens.

Consider the brilliance of a new star. See tender blades of plants peeking through the earth. Hear a newborn's lusty bellow. Watch the unsteady rocking of an hour-old, as-yet-uncoordinated fawn. Nothing shows growth so clearly as the eruption of new life.

In all of life we also see a steady process of transformation, of growth, either positive or negative. Positive growth is marked by greater vitality and function; by contrast, negative growth is marked by senescence and death. Either way, all creation changes, continually.

Growth of a positive nature is characterized by five common features: (1) time requirement, (2) change in size, (3) differentiation in structure, (4) change in form, and (5) sequential progression (order). These features can be observed whether we look at the plant world, the animal world, or at God's crowning creation, man.* First one aspect of growth, and then another, may be more pronounced at any given time in the organism's development, but each will be prominent at some point in the growth cycle.

In the plant world a gardener like myself has ample opportunity to observe each of these features. And no matter how many times I have watched it, growth amazes me. From the moment plants peep through the ground, they change in size and form. Uneven heaving of the spring earth presages the appearance of rows of little leafy arms thrust skyward, as if praising the Lord.

I never cease to marvel as the plants grow to maturity in orderly sequence. They confirm God's early statement that every living creature would "bring forth abundantly, after their kind" (Gen. 1:21). They also follow the sequence described by Jesus: "First the blade, then the ear, after that the full corn in the ear" (Mark 4:28). First leaves, then stems; next blooms and finally fruit—all after their kind and all in God's order.

For me, the hardest part of gardening is waiting. From the moment the seeds go in the ground until the plants appear, no amount of praying or exhorting can make them come into sight before their appointed time. Ecclesiastes 3:11 says that God "hath made everything beautiful in his time." He programs growth.

Even the waiting develops fruit in me. It promotes patience.

---

* See Gen. 1:26; Ps. 8:5, 6.

In fact, for those ready for the postgraduate course in patience, I recommend owning a century plant. It blooms every one hundred years!

If the waiting is hard, the harvest is worth it. Anyone who tastes the early yields of the garden can understand why God asks for the first fruits. He commands, "Honour the Lord with . . . the firstfruits of all thine increase" (Prov. 3:9). The first and the best belong to God. He creates the plant, causes it to grow, and gives the increase.

The same principle of growth, that of constant change programed by God, exists also in people. We observe it in all three parts of man's trinity: body, soul and spirit. We will look at growth of the soul and body together, reserving spiritual change for our most extensive discussion. But first we will begin with what and where our spirits are. Then we will see how we develop, and how God transforms us by developing us according to His design that we may grow and bear fruit.

1

What and Where Is Your Spirit?

He that believeth on me, . . . out of his belly shall flow rivers of living water. (John 7:38)

As he entered my office, there was no doubt about it. This Bible-carrying brother, in laymen's terms, was crazy. I pegged him as psychotic, (the technical term for crazy), because his speech did not make sense.

I was even more convinced when the graying gentleman handed me a letter concerning his recent activities. Rambling and mostly incoherent, it abounded with foul language. Although he'd been married for a long time, to a fine Christian wife, he told a tale of falling in love with a thirty-eight-year-old woman who did not match him in age, race, or educational background. He'd been giving her money toward the time when he could marry her, which would be as soon as he could rid himself of his present wife.

He went on to speak of loving the Lord, then of wanting to cast demons out of his wife, in whom I could discern no evil spirits. Moreover, the man accepted his own actions and plans, as well as his letter, as being entirely reasonable. To me, his irrational thoughts and speech marked him as clearly psychotic.

Yet in the midst of this unusual scene, he began spontaneously to speak in "tongues," to which my spririt bore witness. I recognized it as a heavenly language, the Holy Spirit speaking through his spirit and interceding (Rom. 8:26). What was going on here?

While some would like to believe that all psychotic episodes are caused by evil spirits invading the believer, such is *not* the case. Jesus himself recognized different reasons for illness, only one of which was demon spirits (see those listed in Matt. 4:24). Many times the person who is psychotic has overexerted his psychological resources to the point where he can no longer cope with the stresses of life. Then the person has to go into his own world, leaving the world of reality. When this happens we say that he is psychotic, *crazy*. Certainly the brother before me was crazy enough in his soul, but his spirit was intact.

From the Scriptures we know that the spirit functions through the soul. When Jesus said, "He that believeth on me, . . . out of his belly shall flow rivers of living water" (John 7:38), He was not referring to the physical "belly."

"Where is your spirit?" I once asked a fellow-believer.

He pointed to his stomach.

Puzzled, I persisted. "Why do you think it's there?"

He quoted John 7:38.

Can't argue with a good, scriptural answer. Except that 'belly,' as it is used here, describes *innermost* being.* This speaks to me, not of the intestinal area, but of the personality, the *soul*. Since the next verse, John 7:39, explains that 'living water' refers to the Holy Spirit, it would seem that God's Spirit flows *through* the *souls* of believers.

This also explains how the man whose soul was irrational, not tied to reality, was able to manifest the Holy Spirit speaking through his spirit.

But it raises a lot of other questions, such as: How is the spirit of man related to his soul? What exactly *is* the spirit of man? Where is it? What does it have to do with the whole man? What's different about it when a person has not been 'born again'?

---

* Vine, W.E., *Expository Dictionary of New Testament Words*.

If we approach the spirit first by looking at the way it works in relation to the ways we expect it to work, we might begin to find some answers to these questions. Consider newly converted Christians who have a lot of zeal. At first. Soon they become discouraged. Their disappointment stems from the naive conception that from the moment they roll off the salvation assembly line, they are completed products.

Certainly, from a judicial standpoint, we are complete when we accept salvation. But we are not manufactured, we are *born again*. Experientially, then, we are "newborn babes" who are expected to grow (1 Pet. 2:2).

Yet, little do we realize, when we are born spiritually, that we have a lot of growing to do, nor do we realize that the same features apply to spiritual growth as to any other kind. Growth always proceeds in: (1) *order,* and (2) *time,* and through changes in (3) *size,* (4) *structure,* and (5) *form.* The changes of growth, however, are hard to imagine happening in something as amorphous as 'spirit.' It's hard, indeed, to draw or paint the spirit in any state of development.

Therefore the idea of spiritual growth depends on our conception of what and where the man's spirit is. That in turn depends on how we perceive our spirits to function, both before and after a spiritual rebirth. This brings up the question of how our spirits relate to God's Spirit.

In the case of my patient who exhibited psychotic behavior but spoke in tongues with an air of assurance and faith, the Spirit of God apparently stayed in touch with his spirit and worked through it even though his soul was ill. With treatment and rest the man would get better, and perhaps the incipient spiritual growth which this manifestation of the Holy Spirit implied would cause a spurt of growth within his return to mental health.

We could even postulate in what ways he would grow. Once we have some notion of what and where the human spirit is, how it functions and how it grows, we could, at any rate, build a 'model' of spiritual growth.

Body, Soul, Spirit

People have puzzled over how humans can relate to God who is "a Spirit" (John 4:24). This puzzlement leads to a search for understanding how man functions. To account for the fact that man relates to his environment in three ways—physically, emotionally/intellectually, and spiritually—some searchers have postulated that different parts of man's functioning—body, soul and spirit—are responsible. In this search, a trichotomous-dichotomous debate has sprung up.

Trichotomists contend that man is tripartite. This means that he has three parts consisting of spirit, soul and body. Man, they say, *is* a spirit, *owns* a soul and *lives* in a body. Dichotomists, on the other hand, see man as possessing two parts, *pneuma* (spirit) and *psuche* (soul), with the soul being composed of both body and spirit.

Both dichotomists and trichotomists quote the Scriptures which they believe support their positions. Whichever position one takes, and noted biblical scholars favor each, the confusion seems to be over the function of each part of man. For some, the key to sorting out the problem is found in types of consciousness.

Present-day knowledge suggests that the soul—mind, will and emotions—relates each person to all of his environment. Through the soul we have God-consciousness, self-consciousness and body-consciousness. But these are not three different structures, each functioning independently. Man functions as a unity, not in parts. Wherever he goes, whatever he does, man goes and acts as a unity. His unity, though, seems tremendously complicated. We can simplify our understanding of how man functions by looking at how man's environment is taken into his consciousness.

We know that the body has no knowledge or sensations of itself, except through the brain. We have only to think of accident victims who are paralyzed from the waist down to see the reality of this statement; from the paralyzed area, the brain cannot receive nerve impulses. The person cannot feel sensations in the affected parts of the body. Also, we know that images are picked up by the eyes, but we 'see' with the brain. A person does not hear with his ears, he hears with his brain. All sensations from the body are registered, catalogued and come to awareness in the brain.

In the same way, the personality, the soul, gives awareness of oneself. The sense of 'me,' of self-consciousness, develops over a number of years in what we call psychosexual growth. This sense of myself as a distinct being in my environment registers in my brain.

Self-awareness functions in a mind-body unity which is demonstrated by psychosomatic medicine. It deals with the effect of the mind on the body and the effect of the body on the mind. What I think affects how I feel and what I feel affects how I think. For instance, a person can worry himself into a state of illness. Or the loss of a leg can cause depression. And this physical/emotional interface happens in the brain.

Now, to the mind-body relationship, add the spirit. As we have seen, many Christians believe that the spirit is located in the belly. If 'belly' means 'innermost being,' and if all sensations and knowledge of oneself come to awareness in the brain, could we then say that the spirit of man is also headquartered in the brain?

The solution, I believe, lies in relating the Scriptures to what is presently known about man's functioning. God says of himself, "I am the Lord, I change not . . ." (Mal. 3:6). God's Word concerning man, then, can be trusted as our yardstick, and it should give us the model into which any present or future knowledge about man can be fitted.

Consider the following scriptural passage:

> And the Lord God formed man of the dust of the ground, and breathed into his nostrils the breath of life; and man became a living soul. (Gen. 2:7)

Some believe that the words "formed man" refer to the body; that "breathed . . . breath" speaks of the spirit; and then, of course, "living soul" represents the soul. I believe, however, that this passage does not describe man's spirit.

Instead, this verse tells that God formed a structure for man from inanimate material—"of the dust of the ground." He made man's structure, complete with bones, muscles, arteries, veins, hair, skin, organs, nerves. And brain. Everything ready to function.

But Adam did not function as a living soul until God "breathed into" him, starting the heart beating, the lungs respiring, the brain firing and thinking. Until this time, Adam was a 'soul' in the sense of 'person,' but he was not yet living. God's breath started the life process; it gave function to the structure He had just formed.

As I see it, therefore, the breath of God was not man's spirit, but was symbolic of God's life-giving properties. Man's spirit, the capacity for God-consciousness, is built into his being the same way as his capacity for self-consciousness is built in. Formed as part of his unity, the spirit of man is his capacity to recognize God beyond a mental concept—to form a living relationship with his Creator.

God's breath energized man's spiritual capacity much like plugging a vacuum cleaner into an electrical outlet enables it to work. The sweeper has structure—size, shape and capacity. Until it is plugged in, though, it can't function or perform the task for which it was made. Electricity provides energy for the vacuum cleaner; similarly, God's breath gave function to man's structure.

God planned man's functioning as a whole, but He built it to work through individual cells, each cell having different abilities. Muscles are made of muscle cells. Because of their ability to contract, we can lift heavy objects, or jog, or play the piano. Nerves are made of nerve cells. Their ability to transmit nerve impulses provides lines of communication from the brain to and from other parts of the body. Other cells, made with specialized abilities, secrete hormones which enter the bloodstream and cause certain actions throughout the body. All of these cells have a specialized function.

Other special cells in the brain provide man's consciousness of his world. This is one of the greatest physical miracles. Think of it a moment: your consciousness extends from your internal physical world, such as being aware of your heartbeat, to the farthest star which can be seen. No one has to coach these cells to do their job. That is the role of the Creator. No adolescent woman says, "I'll start my menstrual periods tomorrow." No young man decides, "I'll trigger the need for shaving today!" The Holy Spirit of the Creator has built triggers into our brains for every aspect of our functioning. And each function operates through specialized brain cells.

The consciousness of our environment extends to the ultimate dimension, to awareness of God. Even as some specialized brain cells give us consciousness of our surroundings and of ourselves, those same specialized cells also give us God-consciousness. Through Zechariah God says that the Lord "formeth the spirit of man within him" (Zech. 12:1). God places the capacity to know Him within specialized brain cells.

This capacity is present at birth but it is not operating, even as cells which trigger production of sperm in men and eggs in women are present at birth but not yet functioning. These latent capacities do not function until they are activated at puberty. As for God-consciousness, Jesus said, "No man can come to me, except the Father which hath sent me draw him" (John 6:44). Here, as with every other aspect of man's functioning, the activation comes from God. His Holy Spirit is the activating agent.

Activation of these special brain cells occurs through a two-step process similar to sounding a fire alarm: First, break glass. Second, pull handle to close circuit.

For regeneration, the Holy Spirit first 'convicts,' drawing us to himself while convincing us of our sinfulness. Then we must yield to the Spirit's wooing and "pull our spiritual handle" to close the circuit. When a person truly repents, accepting the salvation offered through Jesus Christ, instantaneous God-consciousness registers in the functioning of those brain cells. Now the energy of the Holy Spirit flows through us. Latent spiritual capacity is converted to active energy.

A similar example relates to a verse in the Scriptures. Until illumination by the Holy Spirit, "the god of this world hath *blinded* the *minds* of them which believe not, lest the light of the glorious gospel of Christ, who is the image of God, should shine unto them" (2 Cor. 4:4, italics mine), and salvation cannot occur. It's like opening the eye. You see instantly when the eyelid raises, activating the appropriate cells in the brain.

When Jesus Christ, the light of the world, shines into us, His energy activates the appropriate structure in the brain.

Returning to Adam, we note that God created an adult man and with His initial breath activated all of his capacities—his sexual and other physical abilities, his self-consciousness and his God-consciousness. In a newborn child, however, not all of these function. The operation of each ability is triggered at different times as the person grows to adulthood. Yet the capacity to function as a *spiritual being,* through the structure of the brain, already exists from birth.

I say 'spiritual being' because some teach that basically man *is* a spirit. I make this distinction because I believe it's more accurate to say that man has as his greatest potential the capacity for living as a spiritual being. In fact, living as a spiritual being is the ultimate goal of his earthly existence. But it appears to me that man basically *is* a personality, a *soul.*

Were man a spirit, it is likely that Paul would have commented, 'Be renewed in the spirit of your spirit.' Instead he said, "And be renewed in the spirit of your mind" (Eph. 4:23), and also, "Be ye transformed by the renewing of your mind" (Rom. 12:2). These words indicate that man's spirit works in his mind and therefore in and through his soul.

Man's spirit, then, is basically a capacity through which a person can have access to God, to form a personal relationship with God the Father through Jesus. Therefore, the spirit of man is not man's essence but an avenue, a channel, through which the Holy Spirit has access for His transforming work.

> The spirit of man is the candle of the Lord, searching all the inward parts of the belly. (Prov. 20:27)

In the same way a candle provides light for darkened corridors, man's spirit provides the means for the Holy Spirit to bring light and thereby to renew 'all the inward parts of the belly,'—that is, all parts of the personality, including the mind, will and emotions.

The location of the Spirit of man, therefore, is in the brain, in those special brain cells which are activated at salvation, among those same cells which give awareness of self as being distinct from the environment. This must be so because only brain cells provide for all types of awareness. As we have said, the brain registers consciousness of the body and its needs. In the brain I am aware of myself and my emotions. And in my brain, the seat of the spirit, I experience consciousness of God.

Therefore, the spirit cannot be located elsewhere in the body. "But," you might say, like my friend who pointed to his midsection, "my spirit is in here because that is where I feel it." Indeed you may feel something there, but it isn't your spirit.

A tremendous number of nerves in the stomach area are gathered into the *solar plexus*. It's the area where a solid blow results in a knockout, a fact known to professional fighters.

> If the Spirit of him that raised up Jesus from the dead dwell in you, he that raised up Christ from the dead shall also quicken your mortal bodies by his Spirit that dwelleth in you. (Rom. 8:11)

Those tuggings may indeed be the Holy Spirit quickening your mortal body, making you aware of His anointing presence in your behalf. But these nerves are the solar plexus, not the celestial plexus. All nerve centers register their sensations in, and take their directions from, centers in the brain. That feeling in your stomach is registered in your brain.

To explain further, we know that different cells have different properties such as contractility, transmission, secretion, hardness, and consciousness. The only cells having the property of consciousness are located in the brain, and these are limited even to specialized locations in the brain. They are not located in the spinal column nor in the legs, arms, or trunk of the body. To have awareness one has to have nerve cells which have this property of awareness. Since they are located only in the brain, in the part which gives consciousness of the body and of self (personality), it is logical also that these brain cells are the site of the spirit.

Teaching that the spirit is located in the abdominal region has created confusion for believers who listen for the voice of the Holy Spirit when praying or at other times. Jesus said, "My sheep hear my voice, and I know them, and they follow me" (John 10:27). Believers cherish this verse when they want to hear Him.

One of my patients expressed confusion and exasperation because she thought, based on the teaching she had received, that the voice of the Lord would originate from the region of her stomach. She had been waiting, straining in vain to hear it from there.

I told her she would hear the Holy Spirit in her mind.

She protested, "I was taught God never speaks to you in your mind," and then she referred to the Scriptures. " 'But the natural man receiveth not the things of the Spirit of God. ... neither can he know them, because they are spiritually discerned' " (1 Cor. 2:14).

I reminded her that "natural" refers to an unregenerated person. Once the spirit is reborn, a person is no longer "natural" but has the capacity through his spirit to receive from the Spirit of God. Man receives incoming spiritual messages in his mind.

God's voice is heard in the mind. The mind functions the same physically in a person who is saved or unsaved; but once a person is regenerated, God speaks *through,* not *to,* his spirit. Speaking through your spirit, the voice of God can be heard in your mind just like any naturally occurring thought. And like Elijah, we too discover that God's voice is not in the strong wind, or in the earthquake, or in the fire: God speaks in "a still small voice" (1 Kings 19:12).

My patient discovered that God had been speaking to her, but she had also been mistaking Him for her own thoughts.

The fact that the Holy Spirit and natural thinking are heard from the same place within explains the confusion in some people who 'heard from the Lord.' Sometimes their 'word from the Lord' is merely some natural desire or inclination. Or it may spring from a lustful desire.

Because they are both located in the brain, the spirit and the soul may seem inseparably linked. Yet God says even they can be divided:

> For the word of God is quick [living], and powerful, and sharper than any twoedged sword, piercing even to the dividing asunder of soul and spirit. (Heb. 4:12)

His living Word, God says, can pass through, dividing soul and spirit. With His Word we can discern what comes from God and what comes from our own thinking.

In later chapters we will discuss this more fully. In this chapter we have been concerned with the location of the spirit of man and why his spirit is not man's basic essence but the modality through which his essence, his personality or soul, can be transformed. We'll explore how a human being grows physically and psychologically, and the ways we grow beyond that natural potential through the operation of the Holy Spirit.

God says we are called to be "conformed to the image of his Son" (Rom. 8:29). Here we have God's word that change in a person is not only possible, but that also He planned for us to be re-formed into the image of Jesus. Once a person accepts Christ as Savior and Lord, the transforming work of the Holy Spirit can begin in that individual's life.

Before we can be transformed, however, we must first be formed. Let's look at how God made us and how we grow.

2

In Wisdom and Stature

And Jesus increased in wisdom and stature, and in favour with God and man. (Luke 2:52)

Physical and Psychological Growth

Anybody entrusted by God with parenthood* knows personally, from the first hectic moment of birth onward, a baby's remarkable progression of physical growth. Measured during visits to the pediatrician, his weight gain is all too soon translated into bulging seams, worn-out britches and too-small shoes. The gurgling, cooing bundle quickly turns into a lusty toddler intent on exploring, mostly by mouth, all the valuable, breakable items within reach. Shortly, he becomes a schoolchild and in turn is replaced by a tempestuous teen-ager.

And so the cycle turns in its appointed round, as Shakespeare recounted nostalgically in "As You Like It":

> All the world's a stage,
> And all the men and women merely players:
> They have their exits and their entrances;
> And one man in his time plays many parts,
> His acts being seven ages. At first the infant,
> Mewling and puking in the nurse's arms.
> And then the whining school-boy, with his satchel,
> And shining morning face, creeping like snail
> Unwilling to school. And then the lover,
> Sighing like furnace, with a woful ballad
> Made to his mistress' eyebrow. Then a soldier,
> Full of strange oaths, and bearded like the pard,
> Jealous in honor, sudden and quick in quarrel,

---

* *Lo, children are an heritage of the Lord* (Ps. 127:3).

> Seeking the bubble reputation
> Even in the cannon's mouth. And then the justice,
> In fair round belly with good capon lin'd,
> With eyes severe, and beard of formal cut,
> Full of wise saws and modern instances;
> And so he plays his part. The sixth age shifts
> Into the lean and slipper'd pantaloon,
> With spectacles on nose and pouch on side,
> His youthful hose well sav'd, a world too wide
> For his shrunk shank; and his big manly voice,
> Turning again toward childish treble, pipes
> And whistles in his sound, Last scene of all,
> That ends this strange eventful history,
> Is second childishness, and mere oblivion,
> Sans teeth, sans eyes, sans taste, sans everything.
> ("As You Like It" II, vii, 139)

In the last line we can sense an air of bereavement, perhaps the same feeling Paul expressed to his beloved Timothy when anticipating the end. Paul wrote, "Demas hath forsaken me, having loved this present world" (2 Tim. 4:10). As Paul and Shakespeare have noted, our mental capacities and our feelings change while our bodies mature. Change is part of living and it is not limited only to our physical bodies. Change happens in our minds and emotions also—in our *souls*.

What Is a Soul?

The soul of a person consists of mind, emotions and will. That's the usual view, and we'll look at it that way. The mind *thinks*. The emotions *feel*. The will *decides*. All function as different aspects of "personality," another word for soul.

Later we will consider the mind, what it is, how it operates, and how it relates to spiritual growth. We'll also be discussing the relationships of emotions to spiritual growth. Just now let's take a quick look at the will.

For the most part, the will has not received the attention it deserves. The will functions in deciding whether a person will act one way or another. With our wills we make decisions about specific behavior.

Without a will we would not be human. Our freedom to choose sets us apart from all of God's creatures. Yet we find that strength of will is often no match for whatever else is working within us. Paul described this difficulty with the will when he commented, "For the good that I would I do not: but the evil which I would not, that I do" (Rom. 7:19). Paul was dismayed that he did not, and seemingly could not, will himself to "do good" consistently. We all experience this difficulty, and our wills determine many of the turns of our lives.

We exercise the will especially in salvation. People *choose* to believe. Romans 10:10 describes it: "For with the heart man believeth unto righteousness; and with the mouth confession is made unto salvation."

To what extent preexistent work on the part of the Holy Spirit affects the operation of the will is not clear in many circumstances. But regarding salvation Jesus said, "No man can come to me, except the Father which hath sent me draw him" (John 6:44). Jesus' statement implies an interaction between the Holy Spirit and the human will in deciding to accept salvation.

But does the will grow? There is little written about the idea. From a common-sense viewpoint it seems likely that exercising the will creates a strengthening effect. Each time a person wills himself to do something, he increases his resolve. In this sense growth occurs.

To many people the issue of free will seems more important than the growth of the will. Perhaps our looking at how growth occurs in the whole realm of the soul will shed some light on free will for those who are concerned. All aspects of the soul—mind and emotions as well as will—intertwine, and one does not work without the others. They function at all times as a unit.

Psychosexual Growth: The Way a Soul Develops

The development or growth of the soul (will, intellect, emotional capacities) over time, which ultimately allows the person to function in an adult male-female relationship, is called psychosexual growth.

The many "models" of psychosexual development which have been propounded have reflected the individual writer's background. By way of explanation, the word "model" as it is used here means something akin to a recipe for cooking. Like a recipe, a model labels the ingredients, the amounts of each, and how they are mixed together to achieve the finished product—in this case psychological development.

Piaget (1954), for example, wrote extensively on the child's developing concept of reality and the factors involved in this development. Lewin (1935), a child psychologist, constructed an elaborate "field" theory—so called because he viewed life as a developing psychological field—to explain behavior. Others explained how man develops, based on observable acts—in other words, what they could see. Since they confined themselves solely to behavior, they quite naturally are called "behaviorists."

Erickson's model for psychosexual development (1950) extends from birth to maturity. At its core is the person's ego, which moves through eight successive stages irrespective of biological age. That is, each stage must be passed through on the way to maturity, even if each is mastered much later in life than is usually the case.

In Erickson's model, the ego is the part of the person's psychological functioning which keeps tuned to the ongoing (what one is doing) experiences of each day. The ego tests what a person perceives. It selects memories, governs action, and otherwise integrates the individual's capacities for orientation and planning.

According to Erickson, the main tasks the ego deals with, in eight successive stages, are: (1) trust vs. mistrust, (2) autonomy vs. shame, (3) initiative vs. guilt, (4) productivity vs. inferiority, (5) identity [Who am I?] vs. role diffusion, (6) intimacy vs. isolation, (7) generativity [leading and guiding the next generation] vs. stagnation, and (8) ego integrity vs. despair.

We will not go any further with Erickson's model, except to say that failure to master the major task in each stage reduces the person's chances of psychosexual maturity.

Freud's psychoanalytic model is the best known. As does Erickson's, it divides psychosexual development into stages, with age approximations for each period. And each stage is characterized by a major developmental task whose successful completion determines the success one has in mastering the task of the next stage.

This step-progression is similar to what happens in the intellect. For instance, mastering algebra enables a person to learn trigonometry, which in turn prepares one for calculus. And all of these subjects must first have the foundation of addition, subtraction and logic. Even though the task for each stage of math is well marked out, it may not be completed until years later. Or never. This kind of delay, transposed to psychosexual development, accounts for immature adults.

Unlike some of the other writers' models, Freud considers not only observable behavior but also man's 'hidden behavior' such as dreams, fantasies and imagination, all of which form important parts of man's mental functioning. Think of it: Without imagination one could not obey God's command to meditate. He says, "This book of the law shall not depart out of thy mouth; but thou shalt meditate therein day and night . . ." (Josh. 1:8). Since a person meditates in his imagination, on the screen of his mind, any comprehensive model would need to include imagination and other forms of mental activity. Freud's model, then, considers man's mental functioning, not just as a simple operation within psychosexual growth, but as a multidimensional process containing conflicts.

Although no model may deal adequately with all questions, because of the completeness of Freud's model we will describe in some detail his stages of psychosexual growth. He named them: (1) oral, (2) anal, (3) phallic, (4) latent, and (5) adolescent. Maturity, of course, follows adolescence and its storms.

(1) *Oral.* The first months of a child's life are marked by multiple feedings, hence the name oral for this initial stage. It extends from birth to about eighteen months and is divided into two parts, oral-receptive and oral-aggressive. In the beginning, the oral-receptive phase, the infant has no teeth. He sucks for hunger satisfaction and for pleasure. During this time he is completely helpless and completely dependent on the parent, usually his mother. He shares with her repeated experiences of his physical care—eating, sleeping, changing diapers, comforting—and the child learns to trust the one(s) caring for him. Learning the parent's predictability and reliability provides a sense of security for the developing infant. His helplessness forces him to *trust,* the main task for the oral period.

Then, as the infant learns to rely on parents and others, he becomes willing to allow the mother out of his sight, learning that her love continues toward him unabated. He learns also to trust his ability to cope with his own urges. Lack in this development of trust seriously interferes with the child's success in relationships throughout his life, and particularly in his later marriage.

The infant feels that the world, and especially his mother, exists for him alone. She is there to do his bidding, to be at his exclusive command. An egocentric, the baby loves himself more than anything in the world. Egocentricity, of course, is a mark of immaturity.

Also, when he is rewarded for learning something new ("Good boy!") the baby often does not understand what led to the reward. He cannot distinguish between occasions when an act will lead to a reward and when it will not. It appears that the child assumes a magical power in his actions which produces the reward.

Then, toward the end of the oral period, the child's teeth erupt, a biological milestone which introduces hazards in his relationship with his mother, especially if she breast-feeds him. Even if not, this oral-aggressive stage changes his previously delightful, slobbery kisses into potential bites, with the natural response from the mother. Handling this period unskillfully can result in the child developing an image of himself as "bad."

In any event, the child learns *causality,* meaning that what he does reaps consequences and that one must be responsible for one's own acts. In this instance, biting results in forfeiture of the pleasure of the parent's comfort. So, in the oral stage of psychosexual development, the egocentric infant learns trust and causality, becoming ready for the next stage.

(2) *Anal.* As he gets older, the child crawls and then walks.

In the anal stage (eighteen to twenty-four months), he deals with the biological complexity of toilet training. How parents relate to this task emotionally affects the child's outlook all of his life.

Some parents are much more strict than others. From this stage comes the extreme emotional control seen in some people ("I have to be in charge or I won't play"). Possessiveness and jealousy arise from this period also. The amount one loves a person can become equated with giving. ("The more you give me, the more you love me.")

Therefore, a poor outcome at this stage of psychosexual development, in addition to controlling behavior, possessiveness and jealousy, is reflected in stinginess and an inability to share. This happens because, rather than being completely passive as in the oral stage, the toddler learns to do more things on his own. His need for autonomy, expressed through exploring and examining, risks frequent clashes with his parents, which means momentary loss of necessary love.

So in the anal stage, the young life grows toward autonomy and sharing. He should now be ready for the next step.

(3) *Phallic.* The phallic stage (forty-eight to sixty months), like the preceding ones, occurs within the framework of interpersonal relationships. The developing child shows increased interest in anatomical differences between men and women. He becomes curious about the origin of babies and the sexual activities of the parents.

The child's affection for his parents, particularly the parent of the opposite sex, peaks at age four and five. His parents' comfort in dealing with the child's sexual interests determines how spontaneous he will be later, and how comfortable he will be in expressing his needs. If parents repress this expression of their offspring's needs by their attitudes, the child may grow up wondering whether his needs and his feelings are appropriate.

Parent-child interactions also contribute largely to the development of the child's conscience, especially in the phallic stage. At the same time these interactions strongly influence the child's comfort with, or fear of, authorities. By the time the child reaches the age of five, his foundations for psychosexual growth have been established, and he goes into the stage which emphasizes intellectual and motor growth.

(4) *Latency*. The latent period of psychosexual growth, from five years to puberty, covers roughly the time from entrance to first grade to the beginning of high school. It is a more placid time than the earlier stages. Rather than learning new tasks, the developing child practices what he has experienced during the oral, anal, and phallic periods.

In latency the child embellishes the things he has learned, adding motor and social skills. Along this line he also learns to adopt different points of view about people. His conscience "grows" too, becoming more principled.

Latency then is a time of integration of successfully, or not so successfully, completed tasks of the preceding stages. It is an active time of expanding social horizons and of practicing the developmental tasks in a variety of settings. Lack of success to this point reduces the possibilities one might have during his lifetime that he will be comfortable with his feelings with others, that he will divest himself of narcissistic self-love, and that he will be able to give to others graciously.

But now, ready or not, physical development in the teen years pushes the person into the storms of adolescence.

(5) *Adolescence*. Adolescence (roughly the teen years) are

those years in which a person establishes his or her identity. The question of "Who am I?" becomes a vital one as the youngster begins forming heterosexual relationships and lasting friendships. It's a time of beginning commitments, of emotional attachments extending beyond the moment.

These identity struggles and new commitments reactivate conflicts from the earlier stages of psychosexual growth. The parents see the teen-ager as "acting childish." He does in fact regress, much like a mountain climber who, having tortuously scaled a rock face, finds himself falling without warning to a lower level. Once again he must traverse the face of the mountain to get as far up as he once was. So it is in adolescence. Or, to draw another picture, the teen-age years are full of sudden shifts of emotion, blowing up like summer storms which are replaced in a little while by emotional rainbows.

The necessity of dependence in a 'grown-up' context, of intimate giving and receiving, so trips up many budding adults that they never successfully attain adulthood. Instead, they remain quarrelsome, brooding adolescents. For those who do reach maturity, however, the rewards are satisfying.

Once adolescence is passed (with the parents heaving sighs of relief) the young adult has laid the psychosexual groundwork for his life. In adolescence he has strengthened his emotional controls and begun to consider others more, a process which continues into adulthood. He launches into a widening circle of social relationships. And he or she is ready for a family in whose setting they can nurture children and together experience life's richness.

We have talked about what happens when a person grows in body and soul, and a little about what happens when this growth is stunted. But that's not the whole story. To achieve full potential, the third facet of each person, the spirit, must grow also.

3

And in Favor With God and Man

But grow in grace, and in the knowledge of our Lord and Saviour Jesus Christ. (2 Pet. 3:18)

Parallels in Spiritual and Personality Growth

In the spiritual, as in the physical and psychosexual realms, we grow also. Our spiritual growth begins with the new birth and follows the same progression that our bodies and souls do. The similarities are so marked that we've heard the comment, "The best way to get a mature Christian is to find a mature sinner and get him saved."

Yet the Christian, no matter how old physically, starts off as a 'babe.' Then, just as in physical/psychosexual growth, over a period of *time* we see a *sequential* progression of *changes* in *form* and *size* and a *differentiation in structure.*

And not only does spiritual growth have the same features as psychosexual development. Spiritual change appears in the soul. Since man operates as a unity, we then see growth in the spirit expressed by the personality. Consider the effect of 'psychological layering' that Paul, by inspiration of the Holy Spirit, outlined in the Word:

> Add to your faith virtue [goodness]; and to virtue knowledge; And to knowledge temperance [self-control]; and to temperance patience [perseverance]; and to patience godliness; And to godliness brotherly kindness; and to brotherly kindness charity [love]. (2 Pet. 1:5-7)

Here we have the sequential appearance of the 'fruits of the

Spirit.' All of them—goodness, knowledge, self-control, perseverance, godliness, kindness and love—show up as changes in behavior. They not only parallel the growth of the personality in measured, orderly changes, but, as we will see, they modify the Christian's soul, his personality.

Change is not easy. Paul calls the Christian life a race, a fight, a war. He says, "Let us run with patience [perseverance] the race that is set before us" (Heb. 12:1). In Second Timothy 4:7, he declares, "I have fought a good fight, I have finished my course, I have kept the faith." And in Ephesians 6:12, he describes the warfare:

> For we wrestle not against flesh and blood, but against principalities, against powers, against the rulers of the darkness of this world, against spiritual wickedness in high places.

Paul implies that we need daily perseverance, continuing commitment and just plain doggedness in the face of the adversary to attain Christian maturity.

The starting gun of the Christian race goes off at the new birth. Here we first experience salvation. To use another example, it's like a national political convention. There's lots of excitement, vigor and commitment. Once the hoopla is over, however, there comes the cleanup and a long, hard road of campaigning to place the honored candidate in office and allow him to reign.

Likewise, placing the Holy Spirit on the throne of the heart doesn't happen without a lifelong campaign. Paul urges believers to "work out your own salvation" (Phil. 2:12), indicating a continuing process. We have plenty of energy and excitement when we are first saved. We make commitments to living the Christian life. But new converts often mistake zeal for growth, and they become disappointed when salvation starts them on a long road of struggle.

They are surprised to find that, rather than happening in a mystical or ethereal way, they must grow in the context of the daily interactions of life. Paul tells us how this works and assures us that we do not have to do it alone:

> Therefore being justified by faith, we have peace with God through our Lord Jesus Christ:
> By whom also we have access by faith into this grace wherein we stand, and rejoice in hope of the glory of God.
> And not only so, but we glory in tribulations also: knowing that tribulation worketh patience;
> And patience, experience; and experience, hope:
> And hope maketh not ashamed; because the love of God is shed abroad in our hearts by the Holy Ghost which is given unto us. (Rom. 5:1-5)

Paul says, in effect, that we can be glad for the hardships. And that the Holy Spirit provides the energizing force which accomplishes our spiritual maturing. Just as muscles grow when exercised, our spirits grow when we are faced with difficulties.

Let's look at the parallels of spiritual and psychosexual (soul) development. For the psychosexual model we will use the six stages of Freud, and for the spiritual model, four successive stages of Christian growth.

BABE: Parallel of Oral and Anal

Spiritual babes show the same characteristics as natural infants. Seldom can babies give, but instead they must be given to. They need constant feeding, attention, touching and protection. We will see how this is true whether they are physical babies or spiritual babes.

In recognition of their voracious appetites Peter urges believers, "As newborn babes, desire the sincere [pure] milk of the word, that ye may grow thereby" (1 Pet. 2:2). The Word of God is meant to be food for the spirit. Paul speaks of it in his first letter to the Corinthians: "I have fed you with milk, and not with meat: for hitherto ye were not able to bear it . . ." (1 Cor. 3:2). Because of the lack of spiritual teeth, babes cannot be fed with solid food for some time. Paul's urging is appropriate for new Christians. They need the pure milk of the Word, just as babies need very simple food in order to stay healthy and to grow properly.

Anyone who has experienced the new birth also remembers both the confusion and the elation the new convert feels. The newborn Christian rejoices in the peace of God (Rom. 5:1), yet he must face a brand-new world. He must learn faith in God the Father in daily living. Faith in the Spiritual Parent (God) equals trust in a physical parent. The realization of utter helplessness in spiritual matters creates in the new believer a need to depend on God the same way an infant depends on his parents.

Initially that dependence has the flavor of passive receptivity. We have observed that God often performs supernatural healings in the lives of newborns. Someone has said that he would rather have new converts pray for him than anybody because God seems to do more for a new believer!

So Christians in the oral stage not only "gobble up" spiritual things; they also trust God implicitly, feeling that there is nothing He can't or won't do for them. Also, like the natural infant, the spiritual babe takes much pleasure in the Parent/God giving him attention. Such self-concern and pleasure-seeking are characteristics of the oral stage, psychosexually, and here we see the same characteristics in the baby stage, spiritually.

The immaturity of the oral stage is also embodied in the magical thinking of baby Christians, who constantly implore God to give them what they want. In their egocentricity, God becomes a Holy Vendor rather than the omniscient, omnipotent, omnipresent Lord of lords and King of kings.* For instance, the popularity of a teaching about making a 'bad confession' in relation to 'getting good things' stems from the immature spiritual child's inability to distinguish what actions bring about desired rewards. The child assumes a magical power in something he has done or that he has seen someone else do, and he thinks that repeating the action may 'pay off' in the same way.

This magical thinking, the result of a lack of knowledge about which action brings results, was beautifully demonstrated at our family table one evening by our six-year-old son. Caught up in the excitement of a beverage company's giveaway contest in which various amounts of money were to be awarded for finding the money designation under the rubber seal inside the bottle top, he fantasized eagerly about how much money he would be given. When his older sister told him she had found a top worth twenty-five cents, he wanted to know where the location of the bottle in the six-pack had been.

"In the middle," she said.

"Next time I'm going to open the bottles in that middle section," he declared. In his magical thinking he naively imagined that, if he did the same thing as his sister, his action would produce the same result.

Many Christians believe that praying in a certain way is certain to give them what they want. But, by definition, imploring any deity to give the person what he wants is magic. God does not share His mind beyond His revealed will contained in the Scriptures:

---

* Packer, 1973

> O the depth of the riches both of the wisdom and knowledge of God! how unsearchable are his judgments, and his ways past finding out!
> For who hath known the mind of the Lord? or who hath been his counsellor? (Rom. 11:33-34)

In those instances where God does speak to a person's spirit, that person can then have "faith in God's faithfulness" (literal translation of Mark 11:22). Beyond that, 'having what you say with your mouth' marks the believer as fixated at the spiritual oral stage. Very young Christians have not yet grasped the truth in Rev. 4:11: "For thou hast created all things, and for thy pleasure [not theirs] they are and were created."

Along this same line, some baby Christians want God never to get 'out of sight,' contrary to 2 Corinthians 5:7 which says, "For we walk by faith, not by sight." They don't want God to get out of their feelings, actually. They've not yet developed an inner knowing that, no matter where they 'feel,' God is, and His love continues in an ever-present stream.

An example of this was a young, Spirit-filled woman, who was a baby Christian. She was coming to me for therapy. One day when she entered the office she began relating her feeling of being upset at the conclusion of our last session. It motivated her, when she got home, to read Romans 8. The last two verses reassured her for a little while.

> For I am persuaded, that neither death, nor life, nor angels, nor principalities, nor powers, nor things present, nor things to come,
> Nor height, nor depth, nor any other creature, shall be able to separate us from the love of God, which is in Christ Jesus our Lord. (Rom. 8:38-39)

Unconsciously, the young woman craved a return to the oral comforts of infancy which had been short-circuited by her mother's psychiatric illness. This passage in Romans speaks to the need of any who feel abandoned or insecure. It gives at least momentary reassurance to baby Christians who may need to feel 'the touch of God' again and again.

Even when more mature spiritually, doesn't every adult at some time or another long to have a physical God? It reminds me of the mother who comforted her young son during an evening thunderstorm. In her most reassuring voice she told him, "Son, there's no need to be scared. God is all around you, taking care of you."

"But, mom," he said, "I need a God with skin!"

This longing on the part of the adult goes back to those physical intimacies from the parent which gave the child warmth and security. Many of the songs believers sing reflect this desire—"Reach Out and Touch the Lord," for instance, or "He Touched Me."

It is also true that development only to the oral phase of spiritual growth explains the believer's fascination with the 'gifts of the Spirit.' In addition to providing the 'touch of God,' the supernatural display seems to enable a dependent believer to command God's power. Sadly, manifestations of the Spirit often serve only to comfort the person through whom they flow rather than ministering to others as intended: "But the manifestation of the Spirit is given to every man to profit withal [for the common good]" (1 Cor. 12:7). The baby Christian therefore delights in evidences of God's presence which minister to him. He is little concerned with the needs of others.

Then, in the stage of spiritual development which parallels the baby anal stage, spiritual pride can be seen. Sometimes a believer 'hears from God' all the time, thus revisiting and savoring the pleasure of feeling that he possesses more favor with God than his brothers and sisters. Obviously, if one hears more from God, God is giving more to the favored one. And God must therefore love him more!

Of course, the Holy Spirit genuinely speaks to the spirit of a believer with reassurance, exhortation, or confirmation of direction. But the Christian in the baby/anal stage may need to believe that God favors him over others, whether his 'word from the Lord' is genuine or not.

Spiritual babies, therefore, need constant protection, both external and internal. Externally they need protection against "the devil, as a roaring lion, . . . seeking whom he may devour" (1 Pet. 5:8). Internally they need protection against "every wind of doctrine, . . . the sleight of men, and cunning craftiness . . ." (Eph. 4:14). In the same way that a mother can be a noxious influence to the baby, spiritual teachers can be dangerous to new believers. Thus the need for internal and external protection.

By His Holy Spirit God protects His own. Because "all we like sheep have gone astray" (Isa. 53:6), God "maketh me to lie down in green pastures" (Ps. 23:2). Like a shepherd watching out for wandering lambs, God looks out for his newborn children.

And First John 4:1 instructs, "Try the spirits whether they are of God." Those who care for young Christians know that it is most important to test doctrine by the Word of God. Until growing believers have matured enough to do this for themselves, they need wise guidance.

A poor outcome of the psychosexual-anal stage shows up later in 'controlling' behavior; such persons are possessive, jealous, stingy and unwilling to share. In the spiritual babe, unchecked spiritual pride proceeds to later legalism, which embodies all of the above elements.

On the other hand, when the outcome of the spiritual babe period of growth is good, the young Christian can avoid many of the pitfalls of the next stage.

YOUNG CHILD: Parallel of *Phallic* and *Latent*

The young child is more capable of caring for himself physically than the baby, but his resources continue to be limited. He needs frequent naps lest he become overextended and irritable. Moreover, he has not yet learned to share with others and may strike out at others in his vicinity, displaying greed, envy and selfishness. The emotions of young children are uncontrolled. To protect themselves, they lie and project blame on others. And the growing independence and curiosity of the very young child can drive his parents to distraction.

I am reminded of the mother who took her two-year-old, a creature half-octopus and half-quicksilver, to the psychiatrist. Fearfully she complained that her offspring must be demon-possessed. After observing the active, robust, exploring child, the doctor dismissed him with a clean bill of health and the comment, "Madam, all two-year-olds are demon-possessed!"

Yet as babies become young children they may show faltering progress. Some do not 'gain spiritual weight.' Alas, many do not grow beyond this stage. They remain spiritual dwarfs and retardates.

Little children feed on adulation. Always seeking approval from external sources, they give to get. And, while they can be allowed to be more on their own, the need for protection remains.

The phallic stage of spiritual growth is marked by an accentuation of dos and don'ts. Exaggerated, legalism becomes institutionalized in the church at this stage. Here a person's maturity supposedly is reflected by specific behavior. We hear questions such as, "Can a Christian drink a glass of wine?" Or, "How many tracts did you pass out last week?" *Doing* becomes the criterion of spirituality.

Legalists overlook the fact that "where the Spirit of the Lord is, there is liberty" (2 Cor. 3:17). Especially do they ignore the *new* commandment, "That ye love one another" (John 13:34). Too often believers measure one another by specific acts rather than by the love they have for one another. Those who so judge have developed only to this stage.

Also characteristic of the young child is the way many believers fear God's punishment if they 'get out of line.' This is not fear in the nature of reverential awe, but more on the order of: 'Will a punitive God possibly tolerate this from me?' This concern becomes threatening in many lives. They feel that God is intolerant and always ready to punish rather than being ever-ready to love.

In spite of the pitfalls, some Christians grow through these stages toward spiritual maturity. In the latent stage they begin to 'get things together.' Integrating the lessons learned before, they begin to serve others. And, having a sputtering relationship with the Lord, not totally committed, they burst into spiritual adolescence.

YOUNG MAN: Parallel of Adolescence

In adolescence, whether psychosexual or spiritual, the question "Who am I?" begs to be answered. Suddenly the maturing Christian is in an identity crisis. He is faced with yielding total dependence on and commitment to the Lord. If he goes through adolescence successfully, he moves from depending on himself and the seen world to total dependence on the Lord and the unseen world. In this he sees himself as belonging to the Lord, who keeps him "as the apple of his eye"

(Deut. 32:10). He understands that he is part of "a chosen generation" whose main purpose is to "shew forth the praises of him who hath called you out of darkness into his marvellous light" (1 Pet. 2:9).

Many spiritual boats wreck on the shoals of self-sufficiency and self-love. Their owners make no commitment of any longstanding nature. To use another metaphor, the runners have dropped out of the race. Or, at this stage the initial army has narrowed like the troops of Gideon.*

But then others, by the time they reach the stage of the young man, have a growing awareness and appreciation of their capabilities. The young man is more discerning, making accurate choices. He actively overcomes physical, academic and emotional obstacles which impede his progress toward realization of his potential.

The spiritual young man has "put away childish things" (1 Cor. 13:11). In the process his vision has become clearer. Giving up more of his self-love, he shoulders responsibility in the kingdom, seeking it first.**

By practicing his authority as a believer, the young man begins to flex his spiritual muscles. The balance between receiving and giving shifts increasingly toward serving others, and he ministers to his fellow man. Now he takes on the role of parenthood.

FATHER: Parallel with Maturity

Parenthood, a joyous experience, brings to fruitfulness one's biological potential. The father stage, marked by ever-increasing responsibilities,*** witnesses a peak in one's capabilities. Early storms characterizing many marriages subside and yield to more domestic peacefulness. The father/mother devotes more time to the priorities of caring for family and business.

---
* Judges 7:2-8
** Matthew 6:33
*** 1 Timothy 5:8

The end point of Christian life is service. Jesus pointed to this goal, the reason one is set apart or sanctified, in His high priestly prayer. He said, "As thou hast sent me into the world, even so have I also sent them into the world" (John 17:18). He further explained His purpose in coming into the world in Matthew 20:28, setting the standard for service: "Even as the Son of man came not to be ministered unto, but to minister, and to give his life a ransom for many." Therefore, we grow spiritually to be more like Christ and, as He did, to serve others.

Perhaps the purpose of Christ in coming to serve others inspired the challenge made by John Kennedy at the Democratic National Convention which nominated him for President of the United States. He said, "Ask not what your country can do for you. But ask what you can do for your country." Maturity shows up most certainly in those who serve.

Many people never attain physical parenthood; fewer yet reach the stage of spiritual fatherhood marked by the maturity of wisdom, of teaching and of caring for the babes, and of tirelessly shedding abroad the love of God.

Those who do are like trees come to full bearing. They bring forth the spiritual fruit of goodness, knowledge, self-control, perseverance, godliness, kindness and love. They are the ones who committed themselves to Christ, and over a period of time have gone on doggedly in the face of the adversary, growing in spirit, coming at last to Christian maturity.

4

But That's Just the Way I Was Born!

The thing that hath been, it is that which shall be; and that which is done is that which shall be done: and there is no new thing under the sun.
(Eccles. 1:9)

A Backward Glance

Those who write about growth but lack the 'salvation experience' central to Christianity do not grasp the quintessence of growth. They do not know its basic source. Any kind of growth—emotional, spiritual, physical—has at its base the ultimate Source. He is God, working through His Holy Spirit. But because each of the three aspects of man's trinity operate by laws common to all, secular writers contribute valuable insights, useful in our study of spiritual growth.

Despite the sadness felt over these secular writers' lack of acceptance of a personal relationship, wherein they could cry, "Abba, Father!" (Rom. 8:15), one need not completely discard their ideas and observations regarding growth. Indeed, many of the definable limits of knowledge about man have sprung from the minds of secular men. For the most part, however, these men's findings are confined to description and understanding of a limited aspect rather than to the integration of the parts which would lead to a better understanding of the process. God revealed much of man's psychological workings to them, but spiritual blindness* prevented them from integrating these parts for an overall understanding. Man has

---
* 2 Cor. 4:4

often been viewed as either *psyche* (soul/mind) or *soma* (body) rather than as an integrated whole.

An analogy of this 'parts vs. whole' thinking might be represented by the parts of a stick of dynamite. Without the fuse to carry current, the dynamite does not ignite and explode. It merely remains a latent capacity for change. Without the spiritual current generated by the Holy Spirit, man's spirit also remains merely a latent capacity for change.

In the field of psychiatry, Sigmund Freud, one of God's unconverted chosen people, discovered many of the psychological truths which still form viable parts of his psychoanalytical model. He put forth concepts about mental functioning such as repression, defense mechanisms, drives, the unconscious, the ego and the superego (conscience).

Building on these early beginnings, later writers have used different terminology while not discrediting Freud's concepts. Various psychiatrists caught glimpses of the true vision of man's essence, his spirit, and of its role in spiritual growth. One of these men is Karl Menninger, a well-known and respected psychoanalyst.

In analyzing society's present dilemma in his work, *Whatever Became of Sin?,* Menninger notes the urgent need for greater personal (social) morality as a corrective for many of society's ills. He affirms that much of behavior which people formerly called sin, now is disguised in other terms. Sin has become *crime, war, group irresponsibility; homosexuality, abortion;* and the names of symptoms, such as *overweight,* are used in the place of the names of the conditions themselves, such as gluttony. By recognizing sin as disobedience to divine will, a transgression of God's law, Menninger localizes the greatest source of the problem areas in the psyche. It is the lack of Christianity and of spiritual growth, under whose aegis alone man will achieve a sense of morality.

He chides the clergy for not emphasizing sin, a now almost obsolete word, as the main culprit causing our ills. According to Menninger, they have failed to sound a clarion call for repentance. He thus focuses directly on the underlying cause needing attention. Although he leaves to the clergy the responsibility for salvation, Menninger clearly recognizes the centrality of man's spirit. He gives hope that other similarly trained professionals will reflect and build on this truth in their labors at healing.

Turning now to authors whose works are rooted in a spiritual orientation, we see that Christians agree that the obvious and only starting place for spiritual growth is regeneration through acceptance of Jesus Christ as Lord and Savior.* In addition to this point of agreement, we find three common factors in their writing. They are: The commonality of man's spirit; the effects of salvation on the spirit; and the changes following over time. Beyond these merits, their focus in approaching the growth issue is quite varied.

Arthur W. Pink,** for example, stresses God's sovereignty. The burden is on God, he says, first for salvation, then for the ensuing spiritual growth. Drawing on various Scriptures, Pink emphasizes that "salvation is of the Lord" (Jon. 2:9), not only to impart salvation to a sinner, but first to place the desire. He calls this "pre-salvation illumination": and refers to 1 John 5:20: "And we know that the Son of God is come, and hath given us an understanding, that we may know him that is true." Pink also says God gives us faith to receive: "For by grace are ye saved through faith; and that not of yourselves: it is the gift of God" (Eph. 2:8). Then he says that even one's willingness comes from the Lord: "Thy people shall be willing . . ." (Ps. 110:3); and "For it is God which worketh in you both to will and

---
* John 3:16
** Pink, A.W. *The Sovereignty of God.* Baker Book House, 1976.

to do of his good pleasure" (Phil. 2:13). Pink's primary concern is wherein the responsibility lies for the change rather than either the individual differences converts bring to the potter's wheel (Jer. 18:2-4), or to the mechanics of the change.

Even though believers are "His workmanship, created in Christ Jesus" (Eph. 2:10), in Pink's work one gains the impression that God the Father is a Master Whittler, fashioning bottles along an assembly line. Were this so, once sealed with the Holy Spirit,* all men presumably would function alike. Pink points out the energizing influence, the power God exerts on His children that they may "be strengthened with might by his Spirit in the inner man" (Eph. 3:16). And he points out God's directing influence as well: "He will be our guide even unto death" (Ps. 48:14). But then, Pink says, God guides us by working in us "both to will and to do of his good pleasure" (Phil. 2:13).

From a different perspective, Watchman Nee,** noted Chinese missionary and prolific writer, conceptualizes spiritual growth as a progressive state of brokenness. For him, the spirit is the "inner man" (Eph. 3:16); the soul is the "outward man" (2 Cor. 4:16). The basic difficulty of a servant of God lies in the failure of the inward man to break through the outward man. The secret to an increased capacity to serve (spiritual growth?) lies in the releasing of the Spirit through the outward man, the thoughts, emotions and will.

Brokenness, says Nee, occurs in two ways, suddenly or gradually. Failure for progressive brokenness lies in self-love and failure to recognize God's hand providing opportunities through circumstances in one's life. Hence, one does have responsibility to respond appropriately to God's circumstances in order for spiritual growth to occur. Spiritual growth is the extent to which one's spirit motivates, or flows through, the

---

* Eph. 1:13
** Nee, Watchman. *The Release of the Spirit.* Sure Foundation, 1965.

outward man in relating to other people.

From the thrust of their works one might speculate, correctly, that neither Pink nor Nee had in-depth training in the psychological sciences. Their training was primarily as theologians. Therefore, their works offer illumination on spiritual growth from theological viewpoints without addressing the functional details of personality change.

Spirit-Controlled Temperament

Christian psychologists have also grappled with this issue of understanding and describing spiritual growth. The 1966 work by Tim LaHaye, *The Spirit-Controlled Temperament,* is a noted work of this type. Because of its popularity, we will look at his ideas in some detail.

His focus is twofold: LaHaye describes man's presalvation psychological differences, and he explains how these differences are modified through salvation.

LaHaye lists four types of temperaments. As a God-given, inborn combination of traits passed through heredity, each temperament is a static, completely developed property at birth. Major contributions to each person's temperament derive from his parents, with lesser influences being contributed by the grandparents. The further a person is removed from his progenitors, the less they contribute to his temperament. The grandparents contribute more than the great-grandparents, and so on.

From this perspective, one's temperament is an inherited weakness. LaHaye makes the inherited temperament equivalent to the 'natural man' or the 'old man' of the Scriptures. Also, temperament may be somewhat hidden underneath the personality, which LaHaye defines as the 'face' we show to the world. And, although he says that inherited temperament has both strengths and weaknesses, he says that the basic temperament needs change through spiritual growth, which he equates with "the infilling of the Holy Spirit." He then describes the process of spiritual growth or temperament change as replacing weaknesses with spiritual fruits.

LaHaye's work, although it has merits, has some serious limitations. First, in my view his theory of inherited weakness as part of an inherited personality type or temperament does not adequately define the old sin nature. Second, the word *personality* has a broader meaning to me than just the face we present to the world. And third, spiritual growth is far more than replacing weaknesses with spiritual fruits.

Limitations of Spirit-Controlled Temperament

LaHaye's concept of Spirit-controlled temperament presents some difficulties for the student of spiritual/personality growth. While the system of four basic temperaments categorizes observable differences, it does not explain satisfactorily the origin of these differences. For one thing, the idea based on physical characteristics, stemming from ancient 'humors'—body fluids—as described by Hippocrates can hardly predict human behavior accurately. In this sense, the concept of temperaments according to LaHaye has no more predictive value than astrology charts.

Also, the idea of an inherited, fixed temperament no longer is given credence. Contemporary theories of personality recognize the role of heredity as transmitter of certain human potentials such as intelligence, but not necessarily of personality traits. Therefore, LaHaye gives more weight to heredity as a determining factor in personality than we find can be supported by current studies. In fact, he focuses on a whole conceptualization of personality which most people in the psychological sciences do not accept today. The notion of temperaments of man is too limited a concept.

Regarding temperament as the old sin nature, I do not see this as a workable concept either. Considered as a whole, the concept of a basic personality type *does not equate consistently to the old nature.* One reason is that the expression of the old sin nature is invariant and predictable in its direction. Jesus described it:

> That which cometh out of the man, that defileth the man.
>
> For from within, out of the heart of men, proceed evil thoughts, adulteries, fornications, murders.
>
> Thefts, covetousness, wickedness, deceit, lasciviousness, an evil eye, blasphemy, pride, foolishness:
>
> All these evil things come from within, and defile the man. (Mark 7:20-23)

It can be seen from this scriptural passage that the old nature predisposes itself toward self-arrogating behavior.

Personality expression, however, varies widely from person to person. Personality is not one-dimensional, with four polarities. Man is made in God's likeness, infinitely varied and complex. He is multi-dimensional with each dimension having many different levels.

Perhaps the confusion about man's basic personality lies in the concept of "nature." Pink attempts to clarify it this way:

> By the Fall man both lost something and acquired something. Term that something a "nature" if you will, so long as you do not conceive of it as something material. That which man lost was holiness, and that which he acquired was sin, and neither one nor the other is a substance (nor personality trait), but rather a moral quality. A "nature" is not a concrete entity, but instead

that which characterizes and impels an entity or creature. It is the "nature" of gravitation to attract; it is the nature of fire to burn. A "nature" is not a tangible thing, but a power impelling to action, a dominating influence. We speak of a lion's "nature" (ferocity), a vulture's nature (to feed on carrion), a lamb's nature (gentleness). A "nature," then, describes more what a creature is by birth and disposition, and therefore we prefer to speak of holiness or imparted grace as a "principle of good," and indwelling sin or the "flesh" as a principle of evil—a prevalent disposition which moves its subjects to ever act in accord with its distinguishing quality. The person of the regenerate is constitutionally the same as the person of the unregenerate, each having a spirit and soul and body. But just as in fallen man there is a principle of evil which has corrupted each part of his threefold being—which principle may be styled his "sinful nature" (if by that be meant his evil disposition and character), as it is the "nature" of swine to be filthy; so when a person is born again another and new principle is introduced into his being, which may be styled a "new nature," if by it be meant a predisposition which propels him in a new direction—Godwards. Thus, in both cases, "nature" is a moral principle rather than a tangible entity.*

As does Pink, we see the old sin nature as the principle by which the basic motivations of man operate in the unregenerate state; and conversely, we see the spirit as the principle, the channel through which the Holy Spirit acts as the motivator of the regenerate man.

We believe that spiritual growth begins as soon as one accepts Jesus Christ as Savior. LaHaye sees the effect of the baptism in the Holy Spirit as the crucial mediator of these changes. To be sure, Paul commands the Ephesian believers (and by extension, the entire Church) to "be filled with the Spirit; Speaking to yourselves in psalms and hymns and

---

* Pink, A.W. *Practical Christianity*. Guardian Press, 1974.

spiritual songs, singing and making melody in your heart to the Lord"(Eph. 5:18, 19). While from this and other Scriptures it is evident that the Spirit-filled life is the norm desired for Christian living, what becomes of believers who, either because of denominational teaching or spiritual deception,* never receive this "double portion?"** Are they consigned to spiritual retardation and stagnation? Casual observation is inconsistent with such a position.

Without receiving the baptism in the Holy Spirit, many believers' lives give evidence of spiritual growth. Indeed, some show more consistent spiritual growth without this infilling*** than do their charismatic brothers, much to the chagrin of the proponents of the baptism. More zeal in witnessing, for example, is shown by some unbaptized believers than by those recipients of this step of spiritual power.****

How can we account for these inconsistencies? We do not doubt that the energizing effect of the Holy Spirit is the propelling force during the Church Age. Clearly, though, individual differences in both natural abilities and in personality formation in response to stresses must be considered in explaining both rates and direction of spiritual growth. Otherwise, inasmuch as LaHaye sees the nine fruits of the Spirit "overcoming" natural weaknesses of temperament, one must assume that those in the large, non-Spirit-filled portion of the Church are doomed to agonize in their weaknesses.

We must understand that Spirit-filled is not synonymous with Spirit-led. Paul says, "For as many as are led by the Spirit of God, they are the sons of God"(Rom. 8:14). Spirit-led is the implementation of God's will, the *working-out* of the capacity. Spirit-filled *is* the capacity.

Think of the full gas tank of a car. Let us say it represents being Spirit-filled. Although the tank is full, the gasoline

---

* 2 Cor. 4:4 ** 2 Kings 2:9
*** Riggs, 1949 **** Acts 1:8

merely has the capacity for movement. Without the motor running, the gears engaged, and the car going in the appropriate direction, which we could say represents being Spirit-led, the gasoline remains merely a potential capacity. Similarly, at any given time, a Spirit-filled believer may not be walking in the light of the Spirit. His gas tank may be full, but he is not in gear, with motor running. He thus possesses only latent capacities for expression of God's will.

LaHaye asserts that all four basic temperaments (and presumably, all possible combinations) have the common difficulty of lack of discipline. This, he says, will be overcome in spiritual growth by the Spirit-filled trait of self-control. Growth is dependent upon the baptism in the Holy Spirit* whose subsequent manifestation of the fruits of the spirit— "love, joy, peace, longsuffering, gentleness, goodness, faith, meekness, temperance" (Gal. 5:22, 23)—in one's life eventually "cancel out" an area of weakness. While the areas of weakness remain as an integral, unchangeable part of the temperament, a greater amount of the particular fruit, LaHaye says, will "overcome" in the struggle.

It's as if we were constructing the roof of a house, attempting to compensate for or to mask the effects of a termite-ridden, poorly built foundation. Although of shoddy construction, the foundation cannot be wrecked and replaced by sturdier materials and workmanship.

According to LaHaye, following the baptism in the Holy Spirit, the Holy Spirit acts on each temperament to replace an area of weakness with one of the fruits of the Spirit, which develops the person toward spiritual maturity. A specific fruit of the Spirit is thus able to fill any given area of temperament weakness. Lack of homogeneity in manifesting these fruitful areas, LaHaye says, comes from "incomplete abiding" in Christ.

---

* Acts 1:8

LaHaye accounts for spiritual growth and the canceling effects of the fruits of the Spirit by setting the soul and spirit as separate entities across whose boundaries emotions are made equivalent. In some cases, he makes emotions equivalent to the Spirit's fruit. Three examples emphasize this point: First, he says that the first three characteristics of the Spirit—love, joy, peace—are emotions which counteract the common weaknesses of temperament such as cruelty. In a similar vein, LaHaye says that goodness is a cure for depression and gloom; and the peace of God becomes an antidote for worry.

This theory assumes that the ability for spiritual change gained from the filling of the Spirit somehow "cancels out" the soul's capacities. This seems contrary to observable fact. First notice that the nine fruits may be conveniently categorized according to their primary relationship:

Love, Joy, Peace:	Us → God
Long-suffering, Gentleness, Goodness:	Us → Others
Faith, Meekness, Temperance:	Us ↔ Ourselves

But love, joy and peace, the characteristics of our relationship with God, do not cancel out cruelty, because it stems from the soul's anger. Anger is a God-given emotional capacity used in the service of defense. Anger-based cruelty stems from childhood abuse and may need specific healing in order to reduce its expression in relationships to others. I have treated patients who, as far as I could determine, loved God very much. They had His peace, but they could still be cruel.

Consider Al, a thirty-eight-year-old spiritual brother, who presented symptoms of rage attacks occurring on an intermittent basis. As a Christian, he was embarrassed by these attacks which were usually triggered by comments which he interpreted as rejection. Between these attacks, during which he could be cruel with angry words or physical violence toward his wife, Al was quite different. He showered love on others in a thoughtful way, being both peaceful and joyful. Some who had ministered to him previously had considered the attacks to be of demonic origin. But no, Al had suffered at the hands of a rejecting mother who criticized him repeatedly. Much memory healing eliminated this problem of rage attacks.

Similarly, the peace of God is not an automatic antidote for worry, which originates in one's soul. Worry is anger over feeling helpless. It comes from insecurity, originating in one's soul.

There are, in fact, at least three types of peace. First, one can have the peace with God that comes with salvation.* Or he can have the peace of God when he is in God's will. Both of these demonstrate spiritual peace. On the other hand, one can feel peace when he is not chronically angry, and this kind of peace has to do with a state of the soul.

And goodness, another fruit of the spirit, is not a cure for the state of soul we call depression and gloom. Emotional first-cousins, gloom and depression result from non-recognition and from turning one's anger inward, on oneself. Indeed, a person may manifest the fruit of goodness conjointly with a clinical depression.

Emotions in the Context of Spirit-Controlled Temperament

Emotions are capacities in the soul which allow outward expression of mental states such as joyful, happy, passionate or angry. They are triggered by thoughts or memories (permanent thoughts), thereby expressing the nature of these thoughts to the world. Emotions possess dimensions such as duration, direction, control, and intensity.

From experience I know that the soul's emotions can be

---

* John 14:27

activated from the spirit. On one occasion, while praying in the office prior to tackling the day's workload, there came from me spontaneous groanings and deep, racking sobs which, as far as I could determine, had no basis in my ongoing emotional mood. On this occasion as well as on others I determined that the soul's emotions were triggered from the spirit during the time that the Holy Spirit was using me as an intercessory prayer vessel.*

LaHaye asserts that self-control, a fruit of the spirit, will overcome the common difficulty of lack of self-discipline, seen in all four temperaments. This view oversimplifies, seeming to say that no one has self-discipline and that self-control and discipline are synonymous. It should be obvious that many people, even prior to salvation, possess considerable discipline in their lives. Some are the obsessive personalities. Others possess emotional self-control. In some people both may be present. In the case of discipline, we think of the way in which a person orients himself to tasks over a period of time; while in the case of self-control we think of the extent to which a person restrains or expresses his emotions. At least this statement is true when the usual connotation of self-control is considered.

LaHaye views each fruit of the Holy Spirit as "overcoming" a specific temperamental weakness. From this perspective each person becomes divided into traits, instead of being dynamically integrated; and these traits are expressed across all circumstances at all times. Experience, however, indicates that each person may manifest a given trait such as honesty with money at some times but not at others. It might depend on the amount of money involved, how badly he needs the money, who was present, etc. In fact, while some people are tightly disciplined in some areas of their lives, in other areas their behavior starts at undisciplined and goes to sloppy! The range

---

* Romans 8:26

and expression of behavior weaknesses, if by that term one means undesirable behavior, is so varied that the nine fruits of the Spirit cannot specifically be said to "overcome" these behaviors on a one-to-one basis.

Unanswered Questions

In addition to these specific shortcomings, LaHaye's presentation leaves unanswered questions. For example, how does one account for those believers who, despite persistent reading of the Word, do not manifest substantial spiritual growth? This lack of growth over a period of time may be true whether the believer is Spirit-filled or not, thus suggesting that to some extent, at least, spiritual growth is independent of being Spirit-filled. Apparently being Spirit-filled is not the only mediator of spiritual growth. There must be other factors which sponsor spiritual growth.

Could it be that those diligent believers know the Word of God but not the God of the Word?

Another unanswered question concerns the believer's responsibility in spiritual growth. Is the believer *merely* to enter into God's rest?* Is the believer *merely* to abide in Christ Jesus?**

James commands, "Be ye doers of the word, and not hearers only" (James 1:22); and further he says that "to him that knoweth to do good, and doeth it not, to him it is sin" (James 4:17). What is 'doing good'? Throughout the Scriptures, the Holy Spirit urges stewardship—faithful, vigilant, steadfast stewardship. Perhaps one of the most rewarding statements a believer standing before the Lord of lords for his rewards might hear would be, "Well done, thou good and faithful servant: thou hast been faithful over a few things, I will make thee ruler over many things: enter thou into the joy of thy lord"

---

* Heb. 4:1
** John 15:5

(Matt. 25:21). The principle of stewardship, which we assume is a way to do good, implies *action* on the believer's part. He is not a passive recipient of spiritual change.

The acceptance of temperament weaknesses as the explanation for people's behavior leads to a feeling of helplessness and stoicism. When despairing over a specific repeated sin, for example, a person might sigh resignedly, "Well, that's just the way I was born! What can I do about it?" This air of defeat leads to a potential denial of one's responsibility.

Also, in lieu of a dynamic understanding of human behavior and the factors underlying change in spiritual growth, one can easily lay too much emphasis on demonic involvement as the cause for sinful human behavior. Deliverance often has magical overtones in the hands of ministers, applied not unlike the question, "Mirror, mirror, on the wall!"

God says, "My people are destroyed for lack of knowledge" (Hos. 4:6). Our goal is to provide information to prevent the destruction of God's people.

In the first chapters we have introduced the theme of growth in all aspects of creation, and then in each of the three areas of the trinity of man—spirit, soul, and body. Our aim now is to discuss the process of spiritual growth and the mechanisms by which it occurs. We will consider the areas of responsibility of both the Holy Spirit and of the believer and the interface between the two. In order to accomplish this aim, we will discuss man's individual differences which he brings to salvation. Personality and its formation will come first.

5

What's Personality?

My substance was not hid from thee, when I was made in secret, and curiously wrought in the lowest parts of the earth.

Thine eyes did see my substance, yet being unperfect; and in thy book all my members were written, which in continuance were fashioned, when as yet there was none of them. (Ps. 139:15, 16)

Defining personality has proven to be elusive. Because of its multifaceted dimensions, the task is like that of the blind men who tried to describe what an elephant looked like. With the limitations imposed by their blindness, each man grasped a different part of the elephant—a trunk, a tail, a leg. Their descriptions, reflecting their honest but limited perspectives, introduced distortions.

Likewise, the way one views personality is limited and varied according to what aspect of personality the person 'grabs hold of.' Each of us has our individual notions of what personality is. Our ideas come from personal perspectives, from self-image and from what we observe of the effects of personality in the behavior of others.

The diversity of opinions about personality reflects man's complexity. Only God fully understands what we are, because He made us.* Our Designer knows all about our "substance," and He records it before our birth: "In thy book all my members were written ... when as yet there was none of

---
* Gen. 1:26

them" (Ps. 139:16). As complex and different as each of us is, God sees it all.

It's not surprising then that His Word speaks in different ways of man's personality. Depending on where it is mentioned in the Scriptures, the word 'spirit' is often used of the soul or the personality. For instance, there's the story of King David, who with his company came to Ziklag. They found that, not only was it burned, but the Amalekites had captured all wives and children and made off with them, a disheartening fact to battle-weary soldiers. Pursuing them, David's men found an exhausted Egyptian whom they revived with food and water. "And when he had eaten, his spirit came again to him" (1 Sam. 30:12). In this context, 'spirit' refers to physical state, perhaps to rehydration.

In another setting, spirit equals emotional mood. It seems that Naboth refused to give his vineyard to Ahab. "Heavy and displeased," Ahab took to his bed. "But Jezebel his wife came to him, and said unto him, Why is thy spirit so sad, that thou eatest no bread?" (1 Kings 21:5). The heaviness of Ahab we would call depression today. So we see that this account equates 'spirit' with emotional mood.

Along the same line, John warns believers to "believe not every spirit, but try the spirits whether they are of God: because many false prophets are gone out into the world" (1 John 4:1). We understand here that John is not referring to disembodied angels (evil spirits) but to men (false prophets)—in effect, to their motivations. We are to question each teacher's (and pastor's) motives in saying what he says, because in Paul's words, "But though we, or an angel from heaven, preach any other gospel unto you than that which we have preached unto you, let him be accursed" (Gal. 1:8). Therefore it would seem that 'spirit' in the Scriptures sometimes means motivation.

And sometimes it refers to emotional mood or to physical state.

In popular usage, the word *personality* equates with social skill or adroitness. The word denotes interpersonal stimulus value, being implied in such statements as, "He has a good personality," or, "He has an exciting personality," depending on what feelings the person referred to stirs up in others—whether he causes the other person to respond in a positive fashion. Therefore, we judge personality in someone else by our response to him or her. Each of us has had the experience of talking with a stranger and within a few minutes feeling as if we had known the person for some time. We feel drawn to him because of the way he relates to us. On the other hand, some people's reserve seems to repel us by their emotional distance, their aloofness. Sales managers select salesmen on the basis of this 'attractive' dimension of personality. Even the word itself, *personality,* has come to mean attractive.

The word personality also denotes the 'face' (*persona,* or mask) one shows to others. For most people, this usage is confusing, because we respond differently to others depending on the other person involved, and on the circumstances. One would respond differently to his employer, his brother, his wife, his pastor, or his children, reflecting the role he plays with each. Each of us, then, presents a different face to different people.

Another usage of personality takes the impression made by an individual. We say he has an 'aggressive' personality, or a 'submissive' or a 'fearful' personality. This usage presumes that the person typically responds to every circumstance or person similarly.

I believe that an acceptable definition of personality would need to consider the complexity of man's psychological functioning. For this reason, I give the following definition: *Personality is the dynamic organization of those psychophysiological systems which determine the characteristic behavior of each person.* This definition contains key words: dynamic, organization, system, and characteristic—which we will consider in order.

Dynamic: Power in the Personality

The personality is dynamic. It is not static. Even as "the word of God is quick (alive), and powerful" (Heb. 4:12), so is each personality alive and full of power. Just as that dynamic quality in the Word of God produces change, so the dynamism in a person's personality also produces change. Yet the personality parts exist in *dynamic equilibrium*—a state of shifting yet remaining stable.

Let's look at two examples of this 'aliveness,' this psychological energy in action. One will be scriptural, the other clinical.

Israel's first king, Saul, presents an interesting study in the way the forces in his personality produced changes in his behavior. At times, Saul fluctuated from being homicidally to suicidally depressed—he may have been schizophrenic in his basic personality makeup. Insanely jealous of David, Saul not only attempted to remove this irritant by trying to murder David on numerous occasions, but he also attempted to kill his own son, Jonathan. Saul showed widely fluctuating moods and toward the end of his life Saul sought advice from the occult in the witch of Endor. Psychological forces in Saul motivated sinful acts which eventually led to his rejection by God as the king and eventually to his death.*

Psychological forces had a different but powerful effect on one of my patients. A trained, but unemployed television

---

* Sam. 18:9; 18:11; 19:10; 20:33; 28:7.

technician/cameraman, he had received a job offer from a neighboring state. He felt the job was God's way of supplying his need,* but he hesitated to respond. During our session he became aware of internal forces creating hesitation.

An internal barrier blocked him. He had waited desperately for God to "set before . . . [him] an open door" (Rev. 3:8), but his unresolved need to have his mother's blessing kept him from stepping through that open door to take advantage of his opportunity. Although the healthy part of this young man's functioning saw himself as capable and responding to God's provision, dynamic forces in his personality restrained him as much as an external chain-link fence.

These examples show the powerful negative effects of forces within the personality. That power, as we will see in later chapters, can be dynamic in a positive way as well.

Organization: The Structure of Personality

"God is not a God of disorder . . ." (1 Cor. 14:33 NIV). His creation was designed to operate in an orderly, organized fashion. Remember that Jesus said, "For the earth bringeth forth fruit of herself; first the blade, then the ear, after that the full corn in the ear" (Mark 4:28). Plants have their own order and organization. Man also, as God's crowning achievement, is tightly organized in body and mind. As a house, having different rooms designated for certain purposes, is organized around the needs of a family, so too are the psychological forces within oneself dynamically balanced. These forces are organized within 'structures' serving certain purposes for the efficiency of one's psychological functioning. Without organization, there is disunity and inefficiency, even chaos.

Returning to the house analogy, different rooms have different functions (i.e. bathroom, bedroom, kitchen). Just so

---
* Phil. 4:19

is the personality, being in some respects the person's internal house. These personality parts may be labeled with different terms depending on the one who labels. But most people agree on the functions. We will look at personality organization under the familiar names used by Freud: id, ego, and superego; and we will also call them flesh, self, and conscience.

(1) *Id (the Flesh)*. At any child's birth, he is an unsocialized, unsaved bundle of unique potential. Given life by God (John 1:3) for a specific purpose ["Before I formed thee in the belly I knew thee; and before thou camest forth out of the womb I sanctified thee, and I ordained thee a prophet unto the nations" (Jer. 1:5)]. This passage, describing Jeremiah's calling, nevertheless applies generally to all God's creations. Each of us has been ordained for unique accomplishments.

We start out with little more than potential. And needs. Initially the infant seems to have only physical needs. Later we become aware of his psychological needs and how he seeks to meet either in any way possible. Since there is motivation to meet these needs, they are spoken of as *drives*.

The child's main goal is to have these needs met instantly, to have pleasure and satisfaction. This is the child's initial outlook on life and it is called living by the pleasure principle. Little does a young child care who he hurts or deprives as long as he is satisfied. He may try to drop a newborn in an attempt to rid himself of the one who he fears is replacing him. And no matter if the youngster is told he cannot have something, he continues fussing and complaining (á la the children of Israel on the way to the Promised Land), because he wants immediate satisfaction.

A child avoids any discomfort, any pain, any irritation. Or any lack of self-indulgence. He is a potential murderer if anyone tries to take his prized toy. He wants to be contented, and he has no desire to change. A well-known psychologist said in this regard:

> The goal of complete comfort and contentment is one that human beings seldom* reach and cannot long maintain. Human beings have been noted throughout the ages for their brevity of any state of equilibrium that they manage to achieve. (Cameron, 1963)**

Yet the very young child wants to have his need for comfort constantly satisfied.

Aggression and sexual drives are the most difficult drives a person struggles with. There are others such as the need to belong, but the predominant ones, aggression and sex, are particularly difficult for Christian believers. They often just pretend that the drives are not there.

Pushing for satisfaction regardless of the costs to others, the collective drives of the human being are called the *id*. Jesus said, probably with sadness:

> For from within, out of the heart of men, proceed evil thoughts, adulteries, fornications, murders,
> Thefts, covetousness, wickedness, deceit, lasciviousness, an evil eye, blasphemy, pride, foolishness. (Mark 7:21, 22)

Interestingly, all these categories of evil can be broken down by their root cause, either the *aggressive* or *sexual* drives. As the Creator, it is not surprising that Jesus would know and describe the same thing that behavioral scientists later discovered. Having plagued man since time immemorial, these drives are roughly equivalent to the 'flesh,' the 'old sin nature'; and they are the same drives whose expression ousted Adam and Eve from the Garden! According to the doctrine of 'original sin,' these are a part of man from birth.

---

* I would substitute "never."
** Cameron, N. *Personality Development and Psychopathology.* Houghton Mifflin, 1963.

(2) *Ego (the Self).* Following the growth principle of differentiation in structure, the second part of the child's personality to develop is the ego. Although the id is present from the child's birth, the ego forms later. Happily, it does not frustrate and stifle the id. Instead, it selects some appropriate way of gaining satisfaction, rather than allowing the drives of the id (the flesh) satisfaction, without regard to consequences. In so doing the ego takes into consideration the law of accountability.

For example, when a person feels hunger pains, the id wants gratification without regard to consequences; it may urge the person to steal the food. At this point, knowing the reality of stealing might provoke a jail sentence, the ego steps in and seeks to satisfy the hunger by buying, bartering, borrowing, or asking an outright gift of the desired food.

Since it knows the consequences of stealing, the ego is said to operate under the 'reality principle' rather than the 'pleasure principle,' as the flesh does. The ego delays satisfying the pressing drives while it selects those actions which are acceptable. This action of delay is called patience. And patience, interestingly enough, as a fruit of the Spirit, is a product of the reality principle as the Holy Spirit works.

The world around us and the physical limits of our bodies demand the growth of organized functions within the personality such as the ego which is capable of dealing with delay, frustration, and conflict. In these terms, the ego seems in some respects similar to the will, our decision-making function, whose job it is to deny gratification while guiding the person to walk in the Spirit. Perhaps we can say that in our psychological organization the ego enables us to handle the basic drives of the id, turning them into positive or negative action by the strength of our wills.

(3) *Superego (the Conscience).* Next, the superego is differentiated out of the ego (super = above), much like a biscuit squeezed out of a larger batch of dough. The superego or conscience then sits in judgment on the ego. The part of the personality whose major function it is to supply approval or disapproval, self-criticism or self-esteem, the superego keeps psychological order—protecting, governing, and blowing the whistle occasionally to mete out punishment in the form of guilt.

The conscience continually supplies approval and love, or disapproval. Let us look at a few examples to illustrate how the conscience functions in this manner. When you were a child it may have been exciting to steal a piece of candy. It may even have tasted good when you ate it. But afterwards, when you were sitting quietly alone, an uncomfortable feeling came over you. It was almost as if your parents were right in the room looking at you with disapproval, pointed fingers accusing you. That was your conscience in action. It blew the whistle, telling you that you had acted improperly.

And what about the time you lied? Nobody may have known, but that internal policeman again blew the whistle. Commonly speaking, what was happening in both instances was the experience of a guilty conscience. The conscience, from inside you, was making the ego, the self, feel guilt. The person so judged feels tension just like he did when his parents, from outside himself, formerly disapproved of his behavior.

It would probably be more nearly correct to say that the person experiences the sense of a guilty self much as if he were standing before a judge who bangs his gavel and pronounces, "Guilty!" The guilty party then hears the sentence imposed. "Self, that was wrong of you to be greedy, (or dishonest, or whatever). I do not like you for that! I disapprove of you and am not going to love you."

In effect the conscience says, "Self, you cannot have any love!" Because the self is hungry without that self-love which the conscience gives, the way we feel about ourselves is lessened temporarily. We see ourselves in a bad light.

Have you ever tried to borrow money or have you ever applied for a bank loan but were denied or rejected? Did you feel disappointment? Let down? Or maybe even desperate, depending on how badly you needed the money? Imagine the conscience as a gigantic bank containing all the money in the world, but instead of paper currency, the money is love or approval. Each time we do something or even think something, the self applies to the conscience, the mental bank president. We ask how the 'president' feels about the action. If the conscience disapproves, the application for love is denied, momentarily at least. The ego becomes hungry. We feel 'bad' and empty inside.

As the conscience develops, it operates continuously, automatically (as do the id and ego), without any conscious thought. It provides a way of controlling our thoughts and of keeping our behavior within an acceptable range of activities, much like a thermostat which works automatically to monitor the physical environment and to provide the normal range of heat or cold.

The conscience, or superego, is the composite of parental dos and don'ts. A parent telling a child "No!" a number of times in a certain situation, for instance, when he is dishonest, stamps this eventually as a part of his conscience. Later when the person is dishonest he feels badly from within himself, even without the parents being present. We could say the conscience is an internal representative of the parents' characteristic ways of disciplining and reproving the child.

In addition, the conscience represents the effects of the cultural standards which limit behavior. In some groups, stealing is not forbidden, so a person might not experience guilt over this type of conduct. The overly strict parents, those who are constantly saying, "No, no," to the child, can cause the child to develop an overly strict conscience, which in turn causes him to go through life feeling criticized all the time.

Psychophysiological Systems

Within each person there are various systems which either motivate, influence, or modify behavior.

On a physical level there are two systems which we will mention. The first is the hormonal system. It secretes growth hormones, sexual hormones, and a host of other hormones into the body. A second physical system is the immunological. It protects the person against various illnesses. Some authorities feel that one of the big factors in the development of cancer is a disturbance in the immune system. The role of vitamin C in this system is the basis for present recommendations of the vitamin.

Both the hormonal and immunological systems interact with psychological dynamics. On the psychological level, defense mechanisms form a system which helps to determine our behavior.

In the transaction of its daily business of psychological housekeeping, in making decisions, the ego feels anxiety as part of the pressure which comes from controlling the id. The ego says "No!" to the flesh in order to satisfy the internal policeman, conscience. To squelch this painful anxiety, the ego or self develops a set of helpers called ego defenses. Although these are too numerous to be described here, the main defense, repression, will be discussed in a later chapter. These defense mechanisms play an important role in spiritual growth. They act like psychological oil, keeping the ego from getting 'all hot and bothered.' Their aim is to keep the ego from being overly aware of the anxiety, thus allowing it enough comfort to go about the business of selecting appropriate choices of action in day-to-day living.

Characteristic Behavior

For the most part you and I behave in a characteristic, predictable way. This is comforting, particularly in intimate relationships such as marriage, because it allows us to know generally what the other person will do under given circumstances without even thinking about it on a conscious level.

Some people are like "the blessed of my Father," of whom Jesus said:

> For I was an hungred, and ye gave me meat: I was thirsty, and ye gave me drink: I was a stranger, and ye took me in:
> Naked, and ye clothed me: I was sick, and ye visited me:
> I was in prison, and ye came unto me. (Matt. 25:35, 36)

In other words, it is typical of them to be compassionate. Other people typically respond as James and John did when some Samaritans would not receive Jesus. They asked Him, "Lord, wilt thou that we command fire to come down from heaven, and consume them, even as Elias did?" (Luke 9:54). Some people do seem to respond angrily to many situations, so much so that this is their characteristic way of interacting with people.

In whatever way people characteristically respond, they demonstrate the truth of our definition of personality: *Characteristic* behavior is determined by the *dynamic organization* of certain psychophysiological *systems*.

The dynamic aspect is what makes change possible. One of the factors which I see in spiritual growth is modification of the characteristic behavior so that, progressively, it "conform[s] to the image of His Son" (Rom. 8:29). Personality is not static. It is full of energy—more or less harnessed, balanced or out-of-balance, but capable of change.

What kind of, and whether, change occurs depends a lot on our perspective of ourselves.

Self-Image

One important aspect of personality needs mentioning here. It is self-image. Often called self-identity or ego-identity, self-image simply is what a person thinks of himself. Often one's self-image corresponds poorly to the way others see him; that is, others see him in a more positive light than he does himself.

Symonds (1951) describes self-image in four parts: Not only is self-image (1) what a person thinks of himself, but also (2) how a person perceives himself, (3) how he values himself, and (4) how he attempts in various ways to defend himself.*

Each person has defended his self-image at times. Consider the tennis player who secretly harbors an image of himself as a fantastic player, numerous missed shots notwithstanding. Here comes a very playable stroke which he flubs into the net for the tenth time. Notice him looking at his racket, looking for the assumed hole in the strings. He wishes a hole were there, for then he would have a valid reason for missing the shot instead of saying to himself, "I am not what I used to be. And maybe never was!"

Or, consider someone who has been asked to perform on stage, perhaps to sing. Hear the inevitable disclaimer, "Well, you have to remember, I haven't sung in years!" That remark is designed to protect the self-image in case of a flub.

---

* Symonds, P.M. *The Ego and the Self.* Appleton-Century, Crofts, 1951.

Like that of the tennis player, the singer's self-image is inflated; he thinks more highly of himself than reality warrants. Probably everybody does so in some area, because one of a person's needs is the desire for omnipotence to counter the memories of being so helpless during the extended period of childhood.

In most cases, however, the protection is necessary because the person has such a poor view of himself. With the singer, this is the case. Often the person has one conscious view of himself and another unconscious one, and they are quite different. When this is true, he really needs protection from his poor performance in any given area.

Therefore, we see that behavior is influenced by a person's self-image—what he thinks of himself, how he perceives and values himself, and how he defends himself. Self-image constitutes a very important aspect of the dynamics of personality.

Effects of Personality

The importance of personality can hardly be overemphasized. Its functioning can be seen in every aspect of one's life, even in seldom-considered areas. We will look now at how six different concerns are affected in the lives of Christians. They are testimony, ministry, preaching, marriage, interpersonal relationships and relating to God.

(1) *Testimony.* Did you ever stop to think that the believer's personality is responsible for the type of testimony he has?

We have noticed that testimonies can be divided into various categories, depending on the type of "problem" the person was having at the time of salvation; i.e., the particular sin most evident in his life. People rescued from alcoholic problems are often passive, dependent personalities. Drug abuse often denotes schizoid personalities, while the presence of flagrant stealing or gambling (or prison sentence for any crime) often points to psychopathic personalities. Homosexuality* and lust are often found in a certain type of personality. Homosexuality equals feminine orientation in a male; lust equals oral character. When a testimony of physical healing is given, frequently arthritis has been present where repressed anger has been a prominent part of the personality. These, and other less frequently heard testimonies, relate prominent sinful actions to personality structure.

(2) *Ministry.* God saves each person for ministry. Jesus said, "Ye have not chosen me, but I have chosen you, and ordained you, that ye should go and bring forth fruit" (John 15:16). But to what extent is ministry determined by personality? Despite God's ordaining the administrative posts of prophet, evangelist, pastor and teacher (Eph. 4:11), it should be recognized that many pastors are not ordained by God. The Lord does not "call" all pastors, a fact evidenced by the self-report of some of them and of the lack of anointing on the preaching of many. A man's need for security, for power or love, his need to be needed, places many men, even unsaved ones, in pulpits.

Personality intrudes itself dramatically when a person, in response to his own needs, does not heed a specific call to the gospel ministry. For instance, a man's refusal to go into the ministry might be an unconscious rebelling against his parents. He then serves halfheartedly and without joy in some other line of work.

Those who do become called by God as under-shepherds of God's flock have personality characteristics which determine the thrust of their ministry.

---

* Ovesey, L. *Homosexuality and Pseudo-Homosexuality.* Science House, 1969.

(3) *Sermons.* Having had the opportunity to become acquainted with various ministers, it has struck me that the thematic content of their sermons at times has derived from their own dynamics rather than from divine leading. In the case of one very passive and dependent minister, we observed that he had difficulty in asserting himself. And his sermons centered around the theme of fearing God.

In other cases, I have seen churches that are run according to the minister's needs, rather than to supply the needs of the flock. I recall one minister who, having spent many of his previous years as a solitary missionary, continued demonstrating his control over all matters in his present church. He had difficulty in allowing the men of the congregation to assume any posts of responsibility. In effect, his church was a patriarchy.

(4) *Marriage.* Ever hear the phrase "that which God hath put together, let no man put asunder"? It is usually heard in connection with marriage vows. Yet, as I see it, only a small number of marriages are actually sealed initially with the stamp of the Holy Spirit! Think of the marriages 1) involving pairs of sinners, 2) involving unequally yoked pairs (believer/ unbeliever), 3) between saints married while sinners, and 4) between saints who never sought God's will in selecting their mates!

All these marriages were probably based entirely on personality needs. Although for the most part these needs are unconscious, desires that are conscious figure in them also. These might be such things as physical attraction and lust, mistaken for love.

Mate selection most often is made on an unconscious basis because of the need for a 'personality fit.'

The degree to which this need for 'personality fit' dictates mate selection, often with tragic and predictable consequences, was demonstrated by a couple I worked with. They came to me after their divorce.

Parents of one child, they were both young and successful in their professions. They were graduates of a well-known denominational college. Both had been reared in the church and the husband was a P.K. (preacher's kid). Both had been Spirit-filled for a long time.

As the daughter of an ultra-successful businessman, a man of influence within his church, the ex-wife had been indulged and pampered in her childhood years by her father. Consequently, she looked for a man with the ambition to become wealthy. As her assets she offered physical attractiveness and intelligence. The husband, from a dirt-poor background, had succeeded in college through much hard work. An officer in several college organizations, he had a high profile as an achiever. Yet he felt unacceptable inside. His ambitiousness and her looks proved to be their downfall; rather than assets, these were really weaknesses to cover poor self-esteem.

These factors were weaknesses because, in the husband's case, ambitiousness was not a natural part of his makeup. Instead, it was a desperate need to rise above the deprivations of his childhood. He wanted to attain material success, and he shunted "the kingdom of God, and his righteousness" (Matt. 6:33) far to the rear. Thus, the basis for his wife's attraction to him became a liability.

Likewise, physical beauty and her dependence on her father's success were her weaknesses. Like all earthly possessions, physical beauty is temporal and bears no relation to those internal qualities, the fruit of the Spirit. Also, Gen. 2:24 says that "a man [shall] leave his father and his mother, and shall cleave unto his wife." Unfortunately, the father's wealth intruded into the marriage and was one of the factors which caused the daughter's lack of emotional 'cleaving' to her husband. It led to the eventual rupture of the marriage.

People who marry for the wrong reasons, perhaps only for a 'personality fit' without the blessing of God and the maturity to handle the partnership of marriage, may expect much difficulty in the relationship. For marriages made in this fashion, let us not blame God for the frequent poor results,* but rejoice in the fact that "we know that all things work together for good to them that love God" (Rom. 8:28).

(5) *Interpersonal relationships.* Two other important areas in which personality is crucially involved are the extent and quality of: 1) interpersonal relationships, and 2) relationship to God. In the first, people differ widely in the number of people in their circle of friends. Some people always have a large group of people about, and others seldom socialize, isolating themselves despite the Lord's commandment "that ye love one another" (John 15:17). Also, within a wide range of acquaintances, the quality of relationships varies from superficiality to intimacy. Many people are unable to tolerate emotional intimacy, thus resembling human butterflies flitting from relationship to relationship. Such is the case of many people who have experienced three, four, or five unsuccessful marriages.

(6) *Relationship to God.* It is obvious that each person relates to God according to the way the person perceives God. This is true, despite what God says of himself: "I am the Lord, I change not" (Mal. 3:6). One's personality determines how he relates to and views others, including the deity.

---

* Gal. 6:8

Look, for example, at the hysterical personality, a personality 'constellation' frequently seen in females. Female hysterical personalities see men as 'sugar daddies,' father figures to take care of them rather than as adult males relating to them as adult females. In their need to be taken care of, these females relate to God as petulant children would to a human parent. They are exasperated when God the Father does not meet those childish demands.

Other personality types introduce their own peculiar distortions in relating to God.

One of the distortions is 'hearing from God' when the voice is really a person's flesh, his own basic drives within his own personality dynamics. One such experience occurred shortly following my surrender to the Lord's ever-wooing love. To expose others to my newly found, dewy-eyed salvation experience, an airplane load of Christian brothers asked me to accompany them to Indiana where one of them was to share his testimony.

The newness and evangelistic enthusiasm was an exhilarating experience for me. During the time of ministry, I was wandering around chatting with anybody who wanted to 'share the Lord.' Suddenly, a tall, suave, angular and elderly man dressed in white linen sidled up to me and spoke *sotto voce,* "The Lord spoke to me; He is coming on such and such a date!" Chagrined that I had been excluded from the elect circle to whom such information would be revealed, I bemoaned my lot!

But shortly thereafter, while meditating in the Scriptures, I discovered Jesus' departing words to His disciples, "It is not for you to know the times or the seasons, which the Father hath put in his own power" (Acts 1:7). It now dawned on me that this man had not heard from the Lord, but in his desire to look omnipotent in others' eyes, he had "heard" something that no man knows.

A similar example is the evangelist Willie Smith, who prophesied the rapture would occur in April, 1980. Though he had been working toward this day for seven years and had "heard from the Lord," his flesh had deceived him.

Another example occurred in my work with a patient. Previously homosexual, addicted to drugs and boozing heavily, Gene had been delivered from all of these by the Lord over a period of time. Now Spirit-filled, he was finishing college and seeking his ministry. Though 'delivered,' he had continuing problems with masturbation which I determined were related to his difficulties in exposing his feelings. This was a carry-over from a traumatic childhood involving the typical homosexual family constellation, a domineering mother and extremely passive, yet sadistic father.

In his struggle to establish a heterosexual relationship, Gene fell in love and soon was engaged. Both he and Sally felt the upcoming marriage to be in God's will. They experienced that peace which comes from God speaking to one's spirit. As the relationship developed, Gene became more demanding. He wanted Sally to deal with all her personality conflicts because they were interfering with *his* peace of mind. Little did he realize that all human relations stir conflict.

Then the Holy Spirit 'spoke' to him one night, revealing all Sally's weaknesses which, in a later confrontation, Gene demanded that she change. They must all "conform to the Spirit's will," he said.

His anxiety mounted. Thoughts of marriage and of the wedding day itself tortured him until suddenly he broke the engagement, summarily terminating his relationship with Sally and also his therapy relationship.

In a letter, he explained to Sally that it was no longer the Lord's will that they be married. He said the Lord had shown him clearly that she and her problems were bad for him. The Lord, he said, would remove anything out of his life that stood in his way ["and if the Lord doesn't, I will," so his unconscious had reasoned]. The girl was heartbroken. But the point of the story is that the Holy Spirit had fleshly motives attributed to Him again!

What else had happened here? It seems Sally suffered headaches and menstrual cramps when under tension. Anticipation of his fiancee's humanness stirred his anxiety. He realized that in the marital relationship, he must compromise and be considerate of the Holy Spirit's reconstructive work in her life. His fear of failing in many areas, including sexual matters, unconsciously prompted him to stop the relationship. Rather than confessing all these factors, he "heard" the Lord had "changed His will." Relieved of the give-and-take of a heterosexual relationship, Gene said he had been "obedient to the Lord."

But not really, as we have seen!

These vignettes are not presented to deride anyone, but to emphasize the necessity for attributing to the Holy Spirit only what really is the bidding or leading of the Spirit. All too often, when one 'hears from the Lord,' it is really the flesh that is speaking. When a person continues to hear from the Lord in this manner all the time, his personality should be brought under scrutiny to determine what needs are prompting this arrogation of continuous divine availability.

We related these stories also to illustrate some of the personality dynamics which figure in Christian life and testimony. We have discussed in this chapter, then, what the personality is and how it is structured. We've looked at some of the reasons why we act the way we do. In the next chapters we will talk about why our personalities are the way they are; and we will treat more fully the reasons for our behavior and how the Holy Spirit prompts us to change and grow.

6

The Why of Personality

Train up a child in the way he should go: and when he is old, he will not depart from it. (Prov. 22:6)

Its Determinants

In the preceeding chapter we established the importance of man's personality and the directing role it plays in his life. We discussed the various parts of the personality, how they are formed and how they act as an internal system of checks and balances. Now we turn our attention to the determinants of man's personality. The important factors in its formation result in the unique adult every person eventually becomes.

Not many years ago it was held that a newborn infant entered this world at birth virtually as a *tabula rasa,* a waxy pad on which was merely impressed the effects of the world. The results of later studies by behavioral scientists have shown that this position is not the whole truth. Consider the hundreds of ways individuals can differ from one another physically—hair and skin shading, and texture; height, weight; eye color; teeth shape and configuration; length of fingers; shape of ears; fingerprints; and all the possible combinations of these traits. God has placed within each infant the potential for uniqueness, even before birth.*

Man's personality is another way God made each person different from his fellow beings. "Diversity in the midst of similarity" is the way one observer described the richness, the

---

* Ps. 139.

shadings, the various nuances of these differences. What causes the differences, so distinct that one can be labelled diagnostically by them? There seems to be a set of well-defined (and perhaps as yet some unknown) factors which play a crucial role in the formation of man's personality. Let us consider some of these.

Factors in Personality Differences

(1) *Formative interpersonal relationships.* Without question, a child's earliest relationships play the most decisive role in determining his personality. There are three relationships in each person's life which stand head and shoulders above all others in determining the course of that person's life. The first is the relationship to his mother; the second, to his spouse; and the third, to God.

The most important fleshly relationship is that with the mother. In many respects, his parents are the 'reality presenters' to the child during the most crucial stages of growth. The way the mother in particular treats a child in the first few years of life inevitably molds him.

Solomon penned, "Train up a child in the way he should go: and when he is old, he will not depart from it" (Prov. 22: 6). We observe two things in this verse: 1) the importance of early training, and 2) the difficulty in modifying the effects of that training ("he will *not* depart from it"). The home is the cradle of spiritual and emotional training; the effects of that cradle will be seen in the person's life throughout its course, barring later psychotherapeutic intervention via the Holy Spirit.

Some authorities feel the mother's responsiveness toward the child even in the first several hours following birth are crucial to his development. Shafii[*] notes that the eye-to-eye contact a mother makes with her child is the root of a positive

---

[*] Shafii, 1979

and satisfying mother-child relationship. This "memory" forms a type of bonding which is felt as acceptance. Could recognition of this kind of bonding have unconsciously inspired the line in the song, "Oh, I want to see Him, look upon His face"? The importance of eye contact in bonding is something that prospective mothers would do well to discuss with their obstetricians; many doctors routinely do not provide mothers access to their newborn infants during those initial, crucial hours.

I often find it helpful in my psychiatric practice to return to this stage of life for a memory to be "built in"* as compensation for the loss of these meaningful experiences. The most lasting relationship of any nature is with one's mother. God seemed to invest special qualities in that emotional attachment; an attachment that, in many respects, represents the closeness and the dependence His children should have on Him.

As crucial as the initial post-birth hours are, the mother's prenatal emotional attitude also is very important to the child's developing behavior. Spirits of rejection have entered children in the mother's uterus. When she does not want the child, a spirit of rejection, as well as other spirits, may enter, creating the potential for adverse behavior later. Even the mother's serenity or hyperactivity during pre-delivery months can directly affect the child. In fact, virtually the entire mother-child relationship, from conception forward, has a direct bearing on the child's emotional well-being.**

This attachment over the years of dependence creates difficulty in a person who finds it hard to separate himself emotionally, not only from the mother, but from others who represent her, such as the spouse.*** We see this attachment extended also to the desire to depend on external objects, because the first 'object' has been the mother. It may seem cold

---

* McDonald, 1980
** Roden, 1979
*** Bowlby, 1969

and impersonal to describe the mother as an object, but this is exactly what she represents to the infant, both initially and for a long time.

Because she is an object to meet his needs, a baby finds separation hard to accomplish and looks for other objects to depend on. Any parent has observed the same behavior in a small child when the mother goes away. The child immediately reaches for the teddy bear or Snoopy, or whatever object substitutes for mother.

This desire to depend on objects was demonstrated by the whole nation of Israel. They looked to Moses, but he disappeared in the thick darkness on top of Mount Sinai, and "delayed to come down" (Exod. 32:1). Finally they cried out to Aaron to "make us gods, which shall go before us; for as for this Moses, the man that brought us up out of the land of Egypt, we wot not what is become of him" (Exod. 32:1). The people of Israel could not tolerate Moses, their mother figure, staying out of their sight. The golden calf which Aaron made for them became their security blanket. We can see then that the nation of Israel was very immature in their dealings with God.

Separation from the objects/people formerly depended on is a mark of maturity. Jesus constantly commanded separation. Sanctification, the process of setting apart, turns men from the world to eternal things. "No man, having put his hand to the plough, and looking back, is fit for the kingdom of God" (Luke 9:62). The looking-back is a reference to earthly attachments, be they materials or relationships.

The earliest attachment, to the other, is later played out in other relations. How many people have not served God to their fullest capacity because of dependent attachments to their spouses? The spouse complains when they serve God; to appease "Mama," they slack their efforts, and God's Kingdom is the loser. In fact, some men openly call their wives "Mama," unaware of the emotional significance of this term of endearment. This attachment is part of the looking-back, the lack of separation of which Jesus spoke.

A considerable amount of anxiety may be built into the child by the mother during those early years of his attachment. Then, as an adult, he worries about many details of life. Adults who seem to be unhappy unless they are worrying about something are probably victims of a poor relationship with their mothers in those crucial early years.

Worry is really anger. It stems from a feeling of helplessness. The unconscious memory of that feeling can be traced to a relationship with the mother in which they felt insecure or helpless.

We see the importance of the mother-child emotional bonding in Hannah's relationship to her long-desired son, Samuel. Long barren, Hannah promised God that, given a son, she would "give him unto the Lord all the days of his life" (1 Sam. 1:11). Later, when her husband Elkanah went to offer yearly sacrifices to the Lord, Hannah stayed at home. She said, "I will not go up until the child be weaned, and then I will bring him, that he may appear before the Lord, and there abide forever" (1 Sam. 1:22). Elkanah supported what she wanted to do, so Hannah remained and nursed her son "until she weaned him" (1 Sam. 1:23).

Second in importance only to the mother relationship is that of father to child. In Samuel's case, the father added unity to the family structure by supporting Hannah in her motherly care. Knowing full well the importance of these two relationships in the healthy emotional development of the child, Satan attacks marriages and homes with ever-increasing vigor in these last days. A fatherless home imposes extra duties on the mother—financially, emotionally, and spiritually. As priest in the home* and God's representative to his family,** the father stabilizes the family unit by serving as a model for his children.

One of the biggest problems created by the father's absence is the lack of strong modeling for sons. It should be no surprise that one of the biggest problems in Christian marriages in this day of increasing divorce is the lack of strong male leadership to guide homes. The only way a man can be developed is to start with a boy; the only way a woman can be developed is to start with a girl.

The parents exert verbal and nonverbal, overt and covert, conscious and unconscious pressures on a child. These mold him during his formative years. Because a child attaches to his parents in a strong emotional bond, he responds to discipline and love. In fact, this bonding is the leverage which parents have in teaching the child the many thousands of lessons needed for successful adulthood.

The intensity of this attachment can be seen in adolescence with the first romantic entanglements. We call this 'puppy' love, but we should remember that puppy love is very serious to a puppy! This first love really represents a reawakening of those early feelings toward the parents, feelings which are played out now in the context of a heterosexual relationship, with its dependency and all the other aspects of courtship. Not only in adolescence, but during all his life interpersonal relationships will be affected by a person's earliest emotional bonding.

(2) *Stresses facing the child.* The developing child faces any number of stresses in the framework of interpersonal relationships. We define stress as any ongoing circumstance which

---
* Gen. 8:20; 12:7, 8; 26:24, 25
** Gen. 7:1; 12:1; 26:1-3

might stir significant anxiety in the youngster. Some of these belong to any normal mother-child dyad.

For instance, the extent to which the mother denies the child's requests stirs emotional pain in the form of anxiety. The longer a child has to wait for his feedings, the hungrier he becomes. The hungrier he is, the more he cries. The more he cries, the more frustration and anxiety he feels. This pattern is repeated when he has soiled diapers, or is sleepy or lonely.

The extent to which the other allows or prohibits emotional expressiveness in the developing infant is another factor which might become a stress in the mother-child relationship. The more expressiveness is permitted, the happier and more emotionally healthy the child becomes. But the more the mother squelches the child's expressiveness, the more anxious and angry he becomes. These feelings then make a stress which must be countered in some way in order for the child to continue his dealing with the mother. In effect, the child must 'figure out' some way of dealing with his feelings, yet continue to please the mother. Eventually the child may become very fearful of emotional expressiveness, and he will avoid any social situations which may demand such expressiveness.

The stress of emotional losses. Stresses which occur outside the mother-child relationship can be grouped under this heading. Some of these are: 1) death of the parent[s], 2) divorce of parents, and 3) prolonged separation from parents. In our discussion of these we will consider the age of the child when he or she encounters the loss.

A child may be faced with emotional deprivation in the loss of one or both parents. To a milder degree, the child feels a loss when the mother is absent for any reason, say to go shopping. Stress intensifies if the mother goes to work; the child feels a wrenching loss, and the emotional effects of this may never be overcome. Worse yet, permanent loss may be suffered when a parent dies. Or, with the availability of extended travel today, some children lose both parents through accidental vehicular death.

One Spirit-filled adult whom I know faces considerable problems because of the murder-suicide loss of both of her parents when she was just a youngster. Because she feels rejected and deprived of these nurturing sources in the crucial years of childhood, unconsciously she seeks reestablishment of that original family by attaching herself first to one, then to another family in her church fellowship. She wants them to respond to her in the form of buying her clothes, lunches, etc. Although she receives these favors initially from people who seek to love her as adult-to-adult, their attentions never satisfy that unconscious longing for dependence. Repeatedly disappointed in her unconscious desires because no family will continue to relate to her as to an infant, she moves on to repeat the inevitable rejection from another family.

Her CB title, "Georgia Orphan," reflects her self-concept of having been abandoned. In spite of the fact that she has acknowledged the "Spirit of adoption" (Rom. 8:15), her continuing self-concept reflects the strength of her personality distortion. Gradually her need to be dependent on others has alienated her from a succession of roommates and from members of her church fellowship. Stresses she faced through the death of her parents as a youngster have proved crippling.

The stress of divorce. Divorce and remarriage of parents confronts the child with yet another emotional stress as the family unit is broken and reassembled. Under these domestic circumstances the child has to learn to adapt to the new parent, often a new male who begins learning the role of father in the family unit. Any number of patients have commented on the difficulty of coping with this unstable circumstance.

Elise longed for the protection and love experienced from her father before his death when she was a young girl. She retold longingly the shared times with her dad. When her mother remarried, the stepfather spanked Elise often. He slapped her on several occasions before her friends, and generally rejected her. Now as a woman, Elise feels timid and shy. She fears decisions and any type of intimacy with her husband.

The stress of separations. Any child's prolonged separation from the parents, especially in the form either of the child's or the parent's illness, constitutes a marked stress.

One middle-aged patient recalled the childhood loneliness she felt during her mother's repeated psychiatric hospitalizations. Those absences created a tremendous void in her emotional development which was still felt in every aspect of her life.

Another patient recalled the isolation and virtual captivity of her early years, when rheumatic fever affected her heart capacity. Sidelined several years as she watched her playmates romp and play in physical activities forbidden to her, she resorted to fantasy. This was much less effective than developing her social skills in shared play.

Frequent residential moves, such as is common with executives (and ministers), provides poor soil for emotional roots. "A rolling stone gathers no [emotional] moss." One young man, the son of a minister, related repeated moves during his childhood which discouraged long-term friendships. Eventually he found himself almost without any ability to make friends.

We have by no means exhausted the listings of stresses. These anecdotes about death, divorce and separation, and illness, however, should help us to understand stresses as formative influences.

Effect of age at the time of stress. Closely related to these stresses, both within and outside the parental relationship, is the age at which the stresses occur. Like a house under construction, the closer to 'completion' the child is when the stresses are present, the better he will weather them psychologically. For example, a child can deal with stress much better if it does not come during an already stressful developmental time, such as conscience formation, when the child is involved in establishing the boundaries of right and wrong. If his parents are divorced and remarried during this time, he may be disciplined by a stepparent whose right-wrong limits may be far different than those of the departed (deposed?) parent. Wide inconsistencies in such areas create confusion for the child.

The mother's working is much easier for the child in the late toddler stage than for the infant busily engaged in learning trust in this primary relationship. Death of a father, always stressful, would be less stressful at certain ages for sons as opposed to daughters because of the unique role father plays in the psychosexual development of each. A general rule is that, the older a child is, the better stresses are coped with and integrated psychologically, and the less they will arouse overwhelming anxiety.

(3) *Family structure.* The family's size has a definite bearing on the child's developing personality. For any given child, the number of siblings (brothers and sisters) he has will be a

definite factor in his personality formation. This is because each child seems to need a certain amount of time with the mother. He needs to have a period of her undivided attention on an individual basis for his healthiest psychological growth.

Interferences with this need can cause serious personality distortions, such as intense rejection. Because of this need, the mother could be seen as the first 'type' of Jesus for the child, because she provides the psychological 'covering' for the child. Jesus is our ultimate Covering.* The most common interference in the mother-child bond is the birth of a younger sibling whom the infant sees as an intrusion into his psychological privacy with his sole possession, his mother. In fact, once pregnancy occurs, the mother's awareness of this growing life diverts her attention inward in anticipation of this new arrival. The developing infant, or toddler, as the age may be, may feel frantic with tension as he senses this happening—his mother pulling away from him psychologically—but he is helpless to remedy the situation.

Several children born within a short span of time means the mother's attention can be less devoted to each child; her relationship to each is diluted. Three children born in twenty-four months means that the first and second children would have had mother's undivided bonding for very brief periods of time. This time period takes into consideration the nine months gestation period for the second and third children. Or, to a lesser degree, relatives such as grandparents, aunts, or uncles, might also be felt as a stress for the child. This happens when these people occupy a great deal of their mother's time, especially if she cares for one who is an invalid. Children under this kind of stress might react by feeling rejected or incomplete.

A young man whom I saw as a patient illustrates this point vividly. Having experienced the joys of salvation and of Spirit-

---

* 2 Cor. 5:21

filled lives, he and his wife nevertheless were having a problem in their relationship which caused the wife to feel that they were being hypocrites. It seems that there was intense, unfounded jealousy on Bob's part. He thought that Jane, his wife, could not be trusted sexually.

We traced the jealousy, as well as an intense need to perform, back to early childhood. He related that his need to perform was so intense that when he had batted a phenomenal .700 in baseball, he was dissatisfied with that achievement. He had not done "well enough." His sexual relationship with his wife was of the same performing quality rather than of loving, giving and receiving.

The oldest of four children, Bob had younger siblings spaced thirteen months, thirty-six months, and forty-eight months from his birth. (Poor mother!) Sadly, Bob had only four months (thirteen minus nine for his sibling's gestation period) alone with his mother psychologically. Feeling deprived because of the advent of the next sibling, he had always felt unconsciously the need to 'perform' in order to regain that cherished position of acceptance, of oneness with the mother.

Because of his lack of critical judgment at that tender age, Bob interpreted the birth of his sibling as an indication that the parents were not pleased with his performance. Hence a frantic, lifelong effort on his part to regain the cherished position in the mother's eyes. Mind you, all this motivation to achieve, this frantic searching for the key to 'return to grace,' was unconscious and solely in Bob's mind, not based on reality. Memory healing through the Holy Spirit replaced his sense of rejection with understanding and with love of himself. Bob's jealous treatment of his wife subsided.

A less well-known factor influencing personality development concerns which particular wife, or several, bore the child.

For example, a man may have been married to three different women, and one of the three may have been his favorite wife. Therefore, children to whom she gave birth might well be his favorites also. This favoritism could not only influence a child's personality but also could sponsor jealousy among the remaining siblings. The Scriptures record such a circumstance: Joseph, Jacob's favorite son, was given a coat of many colors, a gift whose bestowal stirred anger and jealousy among the other brothers.*

Whether the son was oldest or next-oldest made a difference in his rights in a Jewish family. The oldest son traditionally received the birthright for family property and lineage. In the case of Esau and Jacob, Esau possessed the birthright, stirring considerable jealousy in his brother Jacob.** Inability to deal with jealousy, particularly when his mother secretly sponsored Jacob's cause, split the family and caused strife over the years.

So, family structure influences the development of a child's personality. Usually, but not always, the healthiest people psychologically come from a home where they have had the blessing of a loving mother's undivided attention during their earliest years.

(4) *Sex of child.* No doubt about it. Young boys and girls are treated differently. God designed men and women to be complementary in many ways. Woman was made to be man's "help meet" (Gen. 2:18). In order to do this, He made males and females different, not only physically, but also emotionally. These differences are enhanced by the way the child is treated by the parents.

God ordained man to "have dominion over" all living creatures (Gen. 1:28). To do so, man has to assert himself. Thus we can view little boys busily exploring in preparation for this

---
* Gen. 37:3
** Gen. 25:30

God-given adult responsibility. Many parents, fearful of assertiveness, of standing up for oneself, inhibit this type of behavior in their developing sons. This causes boys to be shy and passive as men, just the opposite of what God intended!

The differential treatment begins very early. In studying body contact, Hollander (1980) observed that mothers spend more time holding and cuddling their female infants than their male children. Hollander further states that girls are expected to be cuddly, boys are not. Women—throughout their lives—are more encouraged to express passive, receptive longings. Men, on the other hand, are urged to be active and aggressive. We can see that the way parents respond to their male and female infants plays a large role in helping the individual's personality become what God intends each sex to be.

Homosexuality is a striking example of parental sponsoring of distortions in personality development. Typically stemming from a family constellation of a domineering mother and a passive or emotionally absent father, homosexuality begins to grow when the developing male is cowed repeatedly by his mother. Unsupported by his father when this occurs, the young male becomes very passive and compliant rather than naturally dominant. Later he turns to males rather than females, at whose hands he received the emotional wounding.*

(5) *Ordinal position in family.* One's birth order—firstborn, second or thirdborn, and so on—has long been recognized as a determinant of personality development. Birth order affects a variety of factors such as creativity, achievement, and vocational choice. For instance, twenty-one of the first twenty-three astronauts were 'oldest' or only children.

Birth order also affects sexual adequacy and marriage. Ordinal position in the family bears such a marked effect on

---

* Ovesey, 1969

personality that first-borns are noticeably different from second-borns who, in turn, are dissimilar to third-borns.

Forer* observes that the first child receives in full force the parents' love, standards, attitudes, and values. First-borns tend to be more conscientious, to achieve higher scholastically, and to attend school longer than younger siblings. The oldest child is usually conservative and possesses more self-control. In fact many anxious, obsessive personalities are first-born. They need considerable approval; they're susceptible to social pressure, and are compliant and conforming to accepted standards and authority. Oldest children prefer to avoid conflict and generally need to be in control. They become anxious in situations they are unable to cope with or solve.

The second child tends to be more diplomatic and a good negotiator, having developed skills vis-a-vis an older competitor in meeting his needs. He is generally more friendly and able to maintain better relationships in life than the first-born. Parents favor the second child because he or she adopts different tactics from the more demanding older child. The second child, because his parent's values and standards come to him more diluted, develops devious ways of satisfying needs as opposed to the 'head-on' approach of a first child. The second child is not as competitive as the older sibling, nor is he as attached to external approval as guidance for his actions.

Later children in the birth order (third, fourth, and so on) develop personality characteristics dependent upon the number of siblings. The youngest child is apt to be charming, a good companion, playful and lighthearted. Because he is the baby, with others always around to care for him, he may become very dependent and passively demanding, rather than actively demanding like the oldest child. With an increasing number of children, each successive child has more older parent-surrogates

---

* Forer, 1976

(substitutes). The care of younger siblings often is placed in the hands of the older children to assist the mother. Personality mixtures occur in later children, depending on age differences, sex of the older sibling, parental availability, etc.

The Scriptures record several examples of siblings, among whom are James and John, sons of Zebedee or "Sons of Thunder" (Matt. 4:21; Mark 3:17). Then there are Cain and Abel (Gen. 4:2), Peter and Andrew (John 1:40), Mary and Martha (John 11:5). As birth order would dictate, pairs were quite dissimilar in personality makeup. In view of Forer's finding, it is interesting that Cain, Adam and Eve's oldest son, killed Abel, the second son. It's a shock for the first-born in any family to be displaced from his favored position after a year or so! I have seen many patients whose problem dated to this episode in their own lives.

Based on ordinal position, we could postulate that Andrew, because of his practical, achieving nature* was the first-born. Impetuous Peter** was his later-born brother. Peter's impetuosity showed in his quick refusal to let Jesus wash his feet. He also denied Jesus three times, and he urged Jesus not to allow His crucifixion.

And notice the personality differences between Martha and Mary. Jesus saw that Martha was concerned about achieving: "Martha, Martha thou art *careful* and troubled about many things" (Luke 10:41). She could easily be the older sibling. Mary, meanwhile, seems more sensitive: "Mary hath chosen that good part" (Luke 10:42). She's more loving, more appreciative of her obligation to Jesus. She anoints His feet with expensive spikenard. Mary, the penitent ex-prostitute, might then be Martha's younger sister.

One area of life vitally affected by birth order is the marital relationship. Since it is the most crucial adult relationship for a

---
* John 6:8, 9; 12:22; Mark 13:3, 4
** Matt. 16:21-23; 26:69-75; John 13:6-10

Christian, findings in respect to the role of birth order should be enlightening. Marriage, with all its implications for rearing the resulting generation, is fraught with the peril of divorce. Up to 50 percent of present-day marriages end in divorce. In addressing the question, "Are there certain combinations of persons who may produce a more successful marriage or, conversely, doom it to failure?" (Kemper, 1966), the researcher found greater satisfaction in marriages where: 1) husband with younger sister married a woman with older brother, 2) husband with older sister married wife with younger brother, and 3) husband who was the youngest married wife who was the oldest. Less-preferred marriages, in terms of birth order of the members have both husband and wife oldest *or* youngest, or middle-order husband with older and younger sisters married to woman with older brothers. In particular, the top of the line should not marry the top of the line in another family. Nor should bottom of the line marry bottom of the line.

Of course in considering marriage these findings should not be considered as absolutes, but merely as guidelines. Many other factors beyond birth order are important in mate selection. By far the most important is that the couple have the peace of God* about the other person being His will for his or her mate. Without regard to birth order, God can make "every thing beautiful in his time" (Eccles. 3:11).

Throughout this chapter emphasis has been placed on the factors molding each person's personality. Stress may slow or interrupt the process of personality development. There are times of more intense growth, other times of slower growth. In the latter, the person may become frustrated, feeling that there is no growth at all. However, this may merely be a plateau, a 'standstill' time where previous growth is being consolidated for another spurt.

---

* Phil. 4:9

Personality growth does not just happen. Neither does spiritual growth. There are definite factors which influence both. Growth is a dynamic, ongoing process along with the forces which affect that growth. But there is no widespread knowledge of how the factors can change personality development. To many, development seems willy-nilly; therefore, as parents, they do not see themselves in a position to alter and to help mold their children constructively in a healthy, scriptural manner. How, for example, does one train a child for assertive leadership, or to have healthy sexual attitudes? Or, on the other hand, how is growth distorted? We know these are not just inherited traits or something haphazard; much of a child's personality develops from stresses which act on his day-to-day world.

Authorities in the field of personality puzzle over how to account for personality development in the lives of people whose growth seems inconsistent with expectations. Given certain circumstances, we might predict that a child would manifest unhealthy personality development as he ages. Years later, however, the person may be relatively healthy in his relationships and in the manner in which he copes with life.

In such cases, what has happened? Of course, we do not understand all the interacting effects of the factors which determine personality. Our little knowledge emphasizes man's complexity, which in turn reflects his spiritual heritage. Therefore disproportionate mental health might be accounted for by God working in the person's spirit. No matter what the external forces or natural circumstances confronting and impinging upon a child during his formative years, I believe God can modify or direct growth "according to the good pleasure of His will" (Eph. 1:5). Even as God at His will can induce mental disorder, blindness, and panic* as well as

---

* Deut. 28:28

psychosis,* it is reasonable to contend that the Lord of hosts can induce mental health, even when least expected.

A noteworthy case in point would seem to be Samuel. Because his mother had dedicated him to the Lord, he was left at the tabernacle as a young child to serve the Lord. From this time he was deprived of his mother's love, except for visits year by year. She made him a new coat "and brought it to him from year to year when she came up with her husband to offer the yearly sacrifice" (1 Sam. 2:19). (I wonder, did the Holy Spirit tell her his exact size?) Therefore, Samuel might have been expected to feel deprived and to have had serious personality distortions which could have prevented him from loving his Lord. But Samuel became the circuit-riding judge of Israel, going from Bethel to Gilgal to Mizpah. Upright before the Lord, he served "all the days of his life" (1 Sam. 7:15). The case of Samuel suggests that, while personality is molded by stress, it may develop in spite of pressures which bear on the person.

All of the most desirable determinants of personality do not insure a healthy soul, and all of the least desirable factors which affect personality may not cause adverse effects. The Holy Spirit may, after all, be the most influential determinant of personality.

---

* Dan. 4:32

7

The Windows of the Mind

Behold, thou desirest truth in the inward parts: and in the hidden part thou shalt make me to know wisdom.

Purge me with hyssop, and I shall be clean: wash me, and I shall be whiter than snow. . . .

Create in me a clean heart, O God; and renew a right spirit within me. (Ps. 51:6, 7, 10)

How Mind Affects Personality

As we have been discussing what makes our personalities the way they are, we have said a lot about the unconscious. From what we've said it might seem as though the unconscious mind plays tricks on us. The fact is that psychological functioning and mental functioning are inseparable. Our task in this chapter will be to describe the mind, its levels of awareness and how it works in relation to the personality.

The mind is an efficient structure somewhat comparable to, but much more complex than, a marvelously engineered computer.* Over the years of one's life the mind is taxed with the problems of handling all the person's interactions with his day-to-day world.

Perhaps the mail room of a metropolitan post office might be one way of comparing the mind's tasks. In this bustling mail room, float after float of letters are received. They need sorting and routing, and directory service for those with incomplete addresses. In addition, decisions need to be made for priority

---

* Psalm 139:14

delivery—first class, second class, etc.

In the same way, the mind receives literally thousands of visual (sight), auditory (hearing), tactile (touch), gustatory (taste) and nosmic (smell) 'letters.' They come constantly through the experiences of the person, with himself and with others. Moreover, added to these outside sources are the internal sources such as fantasies, thoughts and ideas. The mind has a Herculean task. It classifies, routes, sorts, stores, recalls, cross-references and compares while also directing the coordination for each day's activities, all somehow without bedlam. God has provided man with a simply marvelous, evolving mind, a structure capable of managing all this complicated activity. And more.

In addition to these complex goings-on, which are handled through innumerable brain circuits, the mind develops 'insulation' against the anxiety stirred up by tremendous industry of the brain and by the push of forbidden desires.

What does insulation against anxiety mean? Anyone who has ever been nervous or tense, common names for anxiety, knows that an awareness of anxiety beyond the normal range is painful. Some people describe it as feeling like they are going to die. That's because of the effects of adrenalin, a hormone, pouring into various parts of the body. It acts like the afterburner which assists a jet plane in a short-field takeoff. A large shot of adrenalin may leave a person shaking and confused later.

Since the continuous awareness and/or the thoughts which trigger anxiety would cause too much confusion and discord, upsetting the smooth working of the mind, it gradually evolves a way of managing this problem by developing the mind's *topology*. The word topology means the outlines of the mind. In an active sense it means the mind dividing itself into, or building into itself, the capacity for different purposes. It works in much the same way as an architect plans different rooms for different functions, and the builder develops his plans. While the bathroom and the kitchen are under the same roof, they are meant for different functions. It's the same with divisions in the structure of the mind. Divisions of the mind function by the *level of awareness one has of the mental contents in each.*

These divisions within the mind which aid in sorting the incoming messages, and thereby reducing anxiety, are the conscious, the pre-conscious and the unconscious. For convenience, the pre-conscious can be lumped with the conscious, giving us two major divisions called the conscious and the unconscious. These compartments or divisions have names which are in common usage, therefore easy to remember. We will include the third division, however, in our discussion.

Let's explore these three compartments and see what each does in a person's life.

Conscious. The conscious contains those thoughts, memories, fantasies and wishes, some extending back to childhood, which can be recalled without any difficulty. From the conscious a person has access to multiplication tables, to phone numbers of value, to names; and here is located his thinking ability which allows him to cope with everyday affairs of life. The psychological contents of the conscious are in continuous awareness, just as one is constantly aware of smells in his environment.

One might visualize these three compartments as a three-drawer filing cabinet, the kind we usually see in business offices. As mental content such as thoughts or experiences (in the form of *memory traces*) register in the mind, they are filed in one of the three drawers by the orderly mental housekeeping of the mind. This process goes on continuously without voluntary or conscious control. The person never says, "Well, I think I will put this in the unconscious! It is too dangerous to think about. And I will let this other thought slide into the pre-conscious." The mind does its sorting without conscious control.

Other parts of the nervous system act in the same unconscious way. For example, we are not in conscious control of breathing or heart rate. The coordination of any physical activity acts under its own controls, with only fleeting, if any, conscious awareness. Imagine what it would be like if we had to think about how to stand or walk every time we wanted to. Life would almost come to a standstill.

So the drawer marked conscious, the top drawer if you will, is open to awareness so that its contents can be examined. All the information from day-to-day experiences which come into the mind is filed in this top drawer initially. For an adult this process of filing, unconsciously, has been underway for years.

Pre-conscious. As with all filing cabinets, the contents of the bulging conscious drawer are periodically sorted through, and some of the contents are filed in one of the other two drawers. Thoughts, fantasies, wishes, dates, numbers and songs—all of these and more—might be placed in the pre-conscious. There they are sorted for recall, but with some effort.

Once in the pre-conscious, the person has less awareness of its presence. Remember that worship service you attended some weeks ago? That chorus that so moved you, the one you sang to yourself for several days afterwards? Then, with the press of other daily mental activity, you quit singing it. Now you may ask yourself, "What was that chorus?" You wrinkle your brow and search through your mental contents. It's still there, filed away in the second drawer, the pre-conscious, for recall. You can find it and sing it again.

See how this drawer of the mind allows ease of recall but yet allows efficient functioning? Since that chorus did not need to be on the tip of your mind all the time while you were busily attending to the details of your life, it was placed in the pre-conscious. It was ready to be found for use again, but stored out of immediate conscious awareness.

Unconscious. The drawer where all classified material is placed is called the unconscious. Here are stored the thoughts and wishes which are confidential—and inaccessible even to yourself. This drawer usually is under psychological lock and key.

If the contents here are inaccessible even to myself, how do I know they are there? We have evidence in slips of the tongue, in dreams, an in other more technical symptoms which we will not discuss at this point. Sometimes this section of the mind is called the *dynamic* unconscious because what is stored there is not just dropped into the unconscious like disposing of wadded paper in a garbage can. Neither do these thoughts just go there by themselves.

Thoughts are placed in the unconscious by a process of *repression.* It takes a lot of psychological energy to retain them there, because they are always struggling to escape. We fear they will cause tumbled havoc like a bull in a china shop. This takes energy away from the person's ability to work. The more material is stored in the unconscious, the more psychological energy is needed to maintain it there, because it is always under pressure to surface. This is why some people feel so tired during the daytime; they are busily fighting this war, without even knowing it!

Some people believe, incorrectly, that they forget thoughts or memories which belong to the past. With few exceptions, however, such as from high fever or operations on the brain or strokes, all mental content is recorded permanently. Much of it is repressed from immediate conscious awareness. Unfortunately the old adage, "Out of sight, out of mind," is not true.

Now imagine the mind as a lake. On top of it float small logs. As they become water-logged the logs gradually sink to the bottom. Suppose we look at the water in cross-section. At any given time logs may be seen at various depths in the lake. However, if we look at the water only from the top view, we might conclude that most of the logs are not there. Once they were in plain sight, floating on the surface. Now they are 'forgotten.' With a huge, long-handled rake we could lift them back to the top for inspection, counting, or removal.

The same is true of thoughts and memories. As time passes they disappear from the 'surface' of the mind. Like the logs, they go to the bottom. But they are put there by repression, completely removed from awareness, in the unconscious.

You might say, "Well, if those thoughts and wishes and memories are in the unconscious, they cannot hurt anything because I am not aware of them." Unfortunately, this is not true. Although unconscious, they retain the same potential for activation, for motivating a person. They are like a seed which, though it has been in a closed pot for years, retains its potential for growth. And does so, given the proper conditions.

James touches on this potential when he says, "Out of the same mouth proceedeth blessing and cursing" (James 3:10). Often the cursing originates from the unconscious and the contents there. Repression's job is to keep all those memories and thoughts in the unconscious, out of awareness, to prevent destructive or embarrassing expression.

Repression and the Unconscious

Repression is the chief of ego-defense mechanisms. It occupies the same role in efficient mental functioning as other mechanisms do, that work beneath the level of conscious awareness to regulate heartbeat and breathing for efficient body function. Repression is not a structure in the brain, not brain cells here and there in different locations; but it is a *capacity* which develops in the growing child. Through repression we are protected from the awareness of some mental content—some thoughts, wishes and fantasies.

For example, a person may covet his neighbor's car, a beautiful Cadillac sitting conspicuously in the driveway every night. Now, to desire that car openly might be more than the person could tolerate, so his repression springs into action. Through repression, the desire to have that car is placed beneath the level of his awareness.

This desire is not the only one which plagues man; there are thousands of unscriptural longings which repression places beneath the level of our awareness. This process begins early in life. It may surprise some to learn that many children, at the birth of a sibling, want to kill the intruder. But repression quickly places that urge into the unconscious so that, while the person has no awareness of the reason, he may 'feel funny' over the years toward his brother or sister.

Repression acts as a dynamic, ongoing capacity, an energy force which scans every person's mental content all the time for those aspects which need to be placed beneath their level of awareness. Some mental content is repressed to the preconscious, some to the unconscious. What mental content is repressed depends on what the person has been taught as a child. If he is not taught it is wrong to steal, he may not repress his thoughts and wishes about stealing. He therefore becomes actively involved in theft. In other words, the energy of repression, programed by experience, keeps our socially and personally unacceptable desires submerged.

As a dynamic capacity, repression takes a lot of psychological energy to maintain itself. It's somewhat like a house when it has been painted. It then needs periodic upkeep to maintain its initial state.

The more emotional content has to be repressed, the more psychological energy it takes to contain the repressed material's struggle to return to a person's awareness. When we live with the constant danger that repressed feelings or thoughts might break loose or surface when we least expect it, we feel anxious and tense all the time. We are afraid we might act on them. This dynamic struggle is sometimes interpreted as an attack from Satan, when it is nothing more than activity in the unconscious.

When Christians say they have given certain feelings to the Lord, they may be quite sincere. But feelings can no more be given to the Lord than your appetite can. They are yours to manage. Only you can do something about your feelings.

Paul commanded, "Wherefore, my beloved, as ye have always obeyed, not as in my presence only, but now much more in my absence, work out your own salvation with fear and trembling" (Phil. 2:12). Paul states that the believer has a responsibility for his own thoughts and feelings. Along the same line, when Peter wrote, "Casting all your care upon him [God]" (1 Pet. 5:7), he didn't mean, "Cast all your responsibilities on Him."

Therefore repression is what we call the capacity God has

built into the marvelous apparatus of the human mind. He deals with this protective functioning in conforming His people to the image of the Lord.* In the Old Testament we can read clear examples of His dealing with repression that short-circuited the accomplishment of His will in the lives of biblical characters. We will present two.

Repression in Biblical Examples

David, a man after God's own heart** had good looks, physical prowess, musical abilities, military skills; and above all, his heart was attuned to God. At God's command Samuel had anointed him king, and David survived Saul's paranoid attacks on his life to become king over Judah and all of Israel. But he consolidated the kingdom only to fall prey to his own lustful desires*** with Bath-sheba. His desire unslaked even then, he arranged the death of Uriah, Bath-sheba's husband, in battle, so that he could possess her as his wife. Bath-sheba bore him a son. "But the thing that David had done displeased the Lord" (2 Sam. 11:27).

To this point David was unrepentant, apparently unperturbed, not feeling guilt over his acts. Why? Because he was repressing thoughts of his deeds. He did not allow himself to feel guilt nor to wrestle with his misdeeds. In his desire to continue temporal pleasures, David pushed any thoughts of his sin into his unconscious. By so doing, the anxiety and discomfort his guilt would have occasioned was eliminated. To break this abhorrent psychological impasse, "The Lord sent Nathan unto David" (2 Sam. 12:1) with a parable about a rich man stealing a poor man's only lamb.

The story shows that Nathan did not confront David right away. Such a tactic would have stirred up David's psychological defenses, causing him to become angry at Nathan and

---

* Romans 8:29
** 2 Samuel 13:14; Acts 13:22
*** 2 Samuel 11:4

to try to excuse his actions. Instead, "David's anger was greatly kindled against the man" in the parable. David declared that the man who did such a thing should "restore the lamb fourfold" and "surely die because he had no pity." Then Nathan replied, with piercing effect, "Thou art the man!" (2 Sam. 12:1, 5, 6, 7).

Imagine how David felt. He was skewered, with thoughts of his deeds and wishes no longer repressed but bathed by the light of the Holy Spirit. He repented then. Repentance brought relief, release from his guilt.* David found a new, closer walk with the Lord, as he tells in his psalms of gratitude.**

Jonah, our second example of repression in the mind of a biblical character, was commissioned directly by the Lord to preach revival in Nineveh.*** He disobeyed. Jonah "found a ship going to Tarshish" instead (Jon. 1:3).

Angry with the sadistic Ninevites for their cruel treatment of his people, Jonah feared for his life at their hands. But he knew that when he preached repentance, God would forgive the Ninevites,**** and then Jonah's anger would be unsatisfied. He wanted the Ninevites to suffer eternal damnation!

Jonah was a prophet of God. His duty was to give God's message, and let God deal with the people. But he repressed both his thoughts of duty and his wishes for the destruction of Nineveh. He serenely boarded a ship bound for Tarshish, in his unconscious probably gloating, "Well, so much for the Ninevites! Serves them right!"

To David, God sent a prophet. To the prophet Jonah, God sent a tempest. It buffeted the ship and spread anxiety. In their concern the sailors cast lots "that we may know for whose cause this evil is upon us" (Jon. 1:7). They [and God] wanted somebody to 'fess up.'

---

* 2 Samuel 12:13   *** Jonah 1:1, 2
** Psalm 51   **** Jonah 4

The lot fell on Jonah. When he admitted his disobedience, the relieved sailors threw him into the sea and the storm abated. Later, from the [disad]vantage point of the whale's belly, and with his wish for the destruction of Nineveh again bared by the Holy Spirit, "Jonah prayed unto the Lord his God" (Jon. 2:1), who delivered him from the whale's belly.

In both of these men's lives the effects of repression are evident. Equally evident in the stories of David and Jonah is the dramatic change that occurs when the unconscious wishes or thoughts are brought into light by the Holy Spirit.

Repression in Present-Day Believers

Now let's turn to present-day believers. What are some of the manifestations of repression and of the functioning of the unconscious in a person's life?

One of these is murmuring against God when He, in His reconstruction work in a person's life, begins to ask for an increased degree of responsibility from that person. God may ask him to bear trials. Contrary to the 'roses without thorns' view of Christianity taught in some circles, the believer's life is one of repeated testings, of drawing the dross* not only for purification but to determine one's mettle.**

God tests His children by tribulations. We should "glory in tribulations also: knowing that tribulation worketh patience; And patience, experience; and experience, hope" (Rom. 5:3, 4). We need not complain when we are tried. God intends it for our good. He wants us to grow.

Repression of material into the unconscious starts early. As a developing infant, each child has the cherished fantasy that, if his parents really love him, they will not expect him to be responsible. They will demonstrate their love always, by taking care of him, by giving in to his demands. They'll allow the child

---
* Psalm 25:4
** Billheimer, 1977

to be dependent indefinitely. So marked is this early fantasy that many children say in anger to their parents, "If my real parents were here, they would not treat me as you do!" Later in life, following salvation, this fantasy has long since been repressed into the unconscious.

Effects of Repression on Christians

Remember, all repressed mental content contains psychological life. It continues to push constantly for open expression. For the most part, and without knowing why, Christians complain when God deals with them. Because they see God now as that parent they once wished to take care of them completely, they are angry if they must take responsibility themselves. I have heard irate patients say, "I don't understand how God could treat me like this, as much as I have loved and worked for Him!" Their unconscious is saying, "If God really loved me, He would not 'do' me this way." The total-dependency wish is still there; unless it is revealed and the person matures, he will continue to relate to God in this manner.

Everyone who has truly experienced 'salvation'—has possessed it rather than merely professed it,* and who has been built in alongside the true Cornerstone**—knows inner peace with God*** through remission of sin and lifting of guilt. Such a person experiences joy and peace. He feels effervescence. The world is a wonderful place and inside him a transcendent bubbling says, "I am loved!"

Indeed, a new love relationship has begun. The intensity of this new love relationship becomes a consuming fire inside the person. It's akin to the emotional experience of adolescent love. Anyone who has experienced puppy love knows that for a short while it blots out the importance of everything else. Soon,

---

* Matt. 25:1-11
** Ephesians 2:20
*** Romans 5:1

however, one settles back to earth. The continuing effects of repression and of material in the unconscious rear their ugly heads.

Similarly, a divorce who remarries may have an initial feeling of well-being. But before long he begins to see spots and wrinkles in his new love. If he's in touch with himself he realizes, "Aha, I am the same old person with the same old internal conflicts and personality problems!"

Following salvation and a honeymoon with the Lord, many people become disappointed when they feel that the Lord has stopped working in their lives. Because, to their surprise, the same problems they have had before with people begin anew. But this is not related to the lack of salvation; far from it, it notes the presence of material in the unconscious that is continuing its struggle for open expression. The battles of sanctification, of *personality transformation* have now begun.

Turning to clinical examples, we will note how each person represses his feeling to different degrees. We will see how unrecognized tendencies toward over-repression can interfere with our relationship to God. This happens more often than most believers would like to think.

Some time ago I saw a young lady who, along with her husband, had recently moved to Atlanta, because of a new job for her husband. They had been in the city only two weeks when her husband's job was terminated.

In relating this news, Lita noted glumly that she had been depressed since learning the startling news. Without knowing why, she had been unable to pray effectively either in English or in the Spirit.* "It's almost like avoiding God," she said.

"What are you really avoiding?" I asked.

Stalling, she responded that both she and her husband were unemployed simultaneously. And, even though she *knew* God

---

* Jude 20

would provide, she was not only depressed; she also was suffering from diarrhea.

I pointed out her anger toward God.

She laughed nervously and said, *sotto voce,* "Lord, look what you are doing to us!"

Once her repressed anger was brought into the light, into her consciousness where she was able to express her anger, she could move toward its resolution. Drawn back into awareness of her Spirit-filled joy,* she reinstituted her prayer life, both in English and in the Spirit.

When people repress anger toward God, they then feel the devil is attacking them and causing their joyless state. As an example of this, another patient related thoughts that her two daughters would be harmed accidentally. These disturbing thoughts she felt must be from the devil. She related some of the events surrounding their youngest years, events which revealed her resentment of the children who were constantly underfoot and kept her pinned down with their demands. This feeling of helplessness stirred anger, which she repressed into her unconscious.

As she continued to free associate to memories of when they were smaller, the Holy Spirit brought other repressed memories to her conscious mind. She had begun to work when the oldest daughter was still a baby. Although it was necessary because her husband was still in medical school, her working caused guilt. She felt that she had deserted her oldest child during a critical period of development.

But now she was able to see the cause of her fears of harm coming to her daughters. She sought forgiveness from her husband for her anger that he had let her down when she had to go to work and 'desert' their daughter. She recognized her anger, stemming from the helplessness she had felt at being

---
* Ephesians 5:19

pinned down by the constant care of her children. Because she acknowledged the anger and its cause, she was able to resolve her anger and the fears which she had once felt were from the devil.

The extent of repression into the unconscious often determines how each person functions in his ministry: "For we know in part, and we prophesy in part" (1 Cor. 13:9, 10). Limited by our humanness, we know in part becaue of: 1) our inability to picture the spirit world except for glimpses God graciously reveals,* and 2) the effects of repression which keeps each person from seeing himself honestly. Repressed feelings can influence the 'flesh' to masquerade in unsuspected ways.

For instance, in some churches prophecies and interpretations are given in public assemblies. In my experience probably 20 percent of these do not spring from the 'heavenly well,' but from the unconscious, from the way people want things to develop.

A story was reported by one of my patients who had attended the service of a well-known local evangelist. During the service the evangelist called out, "Sister, you are sinning [of a certain nature]. If you do not repent in two minutes, the Spirit will depart from you forever!"

Anyone familiar with Scriptures knows that the gifts of the Spirit are not given to condemn individuals, but to exhort and build up the Body of Christ. This message came from this man's anger in his unconscious toward this sister, or toward someone whom she resembled.

This was also true in the case of the young man whom God had marvelously delivered from homosexual practice and drug abuse. We related his case in the preceding chapter, how he was resolving considerable personality problems during the latter days preceding his marriage. His fiancée also was being seen

---

* 1 Cor. 12:10

for other personality problems. Both of these Spirit-filled adults were sure God had spoken to their spirits about His will for this marriage.

One day the man 'knew' that God had shown him many things about his fiancée. God told him that she must submit to his command to resolve all her problems prior to their marriage! This devastated the young lady, and the young man went on to break off the engagement and their entire relationship.

His message, of course, did not come from God. God does not ask one partner to beat up on the other psychologically or any other way. It would be much more in keeping with the character of God if He had told the young man to love his fiancée (and later his wife) while she and God worked out her problems without instructions or demands from the man. The ultimatum he said was from God had originated from his unconscious, from a need to control the situation he so desperately feared.

The Unconscious and Satan

Since the unconscious and the mechanism of repression exert a tremendous influence in each person's life, one of the biggest concerns for any Christian is to distinguish between his flesh and his adversary, Satan. While many examples of the destructive influence of man's own mental functioning have been described, nowhere have we implicated Satan in this functioning. This is because one must first clearly distinguish between how his own fleshly desires motivate and how Satan's wiles and lures affect his psychological functioning secondarily. As in medicine, one needs to make the proper diagnosis so that the proper treatment may be applied. It is inappropriate and wasteful of one's time to rebuke Satan when the problem is in the flesh. Let's look, therefore, at how the unconscious, and sometimes Satan, affects us. We will consider six areas in which the devil and the unconscious may be at work.

(1) *Distinguishing voices.* One of the biggest problems for a believer is in distinguishing the source of the voices, or the internal direction, he 'hears.' Every Christian will hear from three sources, be moved by three motivations: himself, God, or Satan.

Experiencing the glamor and power of the gifts of the Spirit is heady. Throughout history, man has sought power to supplement his sense of physical limits. To many, the *charismata,* the manifestation of the gifts of the Spirit, meet this unconscious need.

The church sometimes finds itself in the same place with present-day believers as early church disciples did with Simon the magician.* Intrigued by the power he saw flowing through the disciples, Simon desired to purchase the power and use it for self-aggrandizement rather than for service. By discernment, Peter clearly saw Simon's motive and rebuked him.

Opening oneself to hear God's voice opens the way for Satan's voice also. It may come via a deceiving spirit. When Christians, seeking a closer walk with God, attempt to find it through the spirit rather than in His Word, they can attest to the problems brought on by mistaking the voice. It is safe to say that many 'prophecies,' 'personal words,' and 'the Lord told me to tell you' messages do not originate from the divine source but from the unconscious. They may come from a desire to be in control, or from one-upmanship or from pride. It is the concern of the Christian believer to discern where his 'voices,' his directions, come from.

---

* Acts 8:1-23

(2) *Guilt.* Before salvation each person has a sense both of personal guilt and of theological guilt. Theological guilt comes from the non-acceptance of Jesus as payment for sin: "For the wages of sin is death" (Rom. 6:23). Salvation should remove completely the sense of theological guilt, because "There is therefore now no condemnation [no judging guilty of wrong] to them which are in Christ Jesus" (Rom. 8:1). But the sense of personal guilt is largely unchanged by the salvation experience.

Personal guilt comes from transgressing moral and/or parental standards. Even though many memories of these transgressions have been repressed into the unconscious over the years, a sense of wrongdoing remains. The unconscious then can be said to create a sense of guilt. But resolving the sense of personal guilt, which often has at its root a feeling of unworthiness, is part of what happens when you "work out your own salvation with fear and trembling" (Phil. 2:12). This is an individual matter for each person, with each one's guilt stemming from different circumstances.

Personal guilt needs to be distinguished from Satan's condemnation. As the accuser of the brethren,* Satan stands before God's throne day and night. He also has access to men's minds with his accusations. His accusations attempt to cast doubt on the person's salvation and/or the course of his spiritual progress.

Following an isolated sinful act, that accusing voice slyly intones, "Jesus will stop loving you for that!" Or, *"Nobody who does that could be saved!"* To the first you could say, "Yes, I sinned. But 'I am persuaded that [nothing] . . . shall be able to separate [me] . . . from the love of God, which is in Christ Jesus our Lord' " (Rom. 8:38). To the second, "Yes, I did slip. But the Word says, 'If thou shalt confess with thy mouth the Lord Jesus, and shalt believe in thine heart that God hath

---

* Rev. 12:10

raised him from the dead, thou shalt be saved' "(Rom. 10:9). Jesus modelled such a reply for us,* skewering Satan by the "sword of the Spirit" (Eph. 6:17). Guilt imposed on us by our consciences should be differentiated from the accusations of Satan. The Word of God can always be used effectively against the Deceiver.

(3) *Interpersonal relationships.* The unconscious determines to a great extent how each person reacts to other people. Remember, I said earlier that all the mental content—fantasies, wishes, thoughts, memories from earlier times which have been repressed into a person's unconscious—always struggles for expression. Even though repression can be successful for the most part in keeping it there, at times the unconscious material slips out in disguised forms in interactions with others. Let me give an example or two.

John had been in therapy for some time when he came in to tell me that he had almost slugged his boss. An insurance salesman, John had sought, and felt he had obtained, permission from his boss to pursue academic courses which would then be tax-deductible. He took a tax exemption on his tuition which was challenged by the IRS. When asked to verify his endorsement, the boss denied he had given permission. At that moment, John became so irate that he almost hit him.

Later, in puzzling over this reaction, he began talking about his father. In John's early childhood the father repeatedly broke promises to John, disappointing him greatly. The anger over these disappointments had been repressed. The incident with his boss caused the anger to 'leak out' momentarily. He transferred the anger meant for his father to another authority figure who had treated him similarly.

Many people respond to their spouses as they wished they

---

* Matt. 4:4-10

had responded to their parents in their early years. A lady told me angrily that over the Labor Day holiday her husband rose early, rousing the entire household, despite their howls of protest. She fought with him about it.

In exploring her reaction, she was able to return almost immediately to repressed feelings toward her dad. During her early dating years her father consistently would not give her an answer about whether she could go out on a given night until shortly before time to leave. It had been a frustrating, controlling pattern of behavior on his part. When her husband gave orders at the last minute, she responded to him as she had wanted to respond to her dad, with anger. The devil may have been operative here—but only secondarily to her unconscious.

(4) *Demonic imitation.* At times the relaxation of repression causes psychic content from the unconscious to pour out in an overwhelming manner, resulting in a behavioral pattern which mimics demonic involvement. In fact, it is often mistaken for this condition. Hardly a week goes by that I don't receive a phone call from a concerned relative about some person in whom this has occurred.

It happens most frequently in people in schizophrenic episodes. The differentiation between demonic imitation and demonic possession is important, because a person can begin acting in an uncharacteristic or unusual manner rather quickly, frightening the onlookers. Let me cite such a case.

Several weeks ago, I prepared to pray over a specific memory with a lady who had had many psychological wounds, particularly those involving her dad's behavior toward her. As I grasped her hands and closed my eyes, the patient began writhing. Then she suddenly stood erect, moaning, and moved into the corner of my office. I had dropped one of her hands, but held on to the other for her emotional support. I was half-dragged with her as she sank on her knees in the corner of the room, ending with her head at the intersection of the walls and floor, obviously in psychological pain, crying with deep sobs.

To an untrained observer, it would appear that she was demonically possessed. Such was not the case. The description of her childhood scene had caused her repression to become incomplete. Thus the full impact of her father's berating and beating her once again scorched her mind, and proved to be more than she could cope with without moving as if to defend herself. After I supported her through this brief episode, we prayed successfully for healing of this memory. The painful psychological impact of this scene would be physically equivalent to dousing a person with a bucket of near-scalding water. One can begin to see how complex the mind is!

Many times, unfortunately, because of similar behavior believers have had evil spirits incorrectly imputed to them. No amount of deliverance would have helped this patient, because her behavior was schizophrenic, not demon-possessed. Knowing the difference between the two diagnoses should raise the level of awareness for all believers; it should also acknowledge the powerful effect of the unconscious in our lives.

(5) *Psychosis.* Closely related to the foregoing category, but usually more extensive and long lasting, is psychosis, which is a mental break with reality. In psychosis a person is, in laymen's terms, 'crazy.' His actions are bizarre and he does not view reality the way others around him do. The uninitiated often feel that psychosis is the result of demonic involvement. But most often it relates to feelings being repressed into the unconscious

over the years and then suddenly being released into consciousness.

Denial and repression of too many feelings is sinful, because the Scriptures command, "Be ye angry" (Eph. 4:26). The overuse of repression over the years can result, with further sudden emotional stress, in a failure of the repression. There's a sudden return to consciousness of the repressed content. Overwhelmed by the psychological pain of these feelings, the person converts reality into psychosis (his own unique reality) in order to survive.

Some people who have been psychotic need deliverance following their return to reality. I have seen and participated in successful deliverance from spirits of anger, rejection, etc. In my own experience, however, psychotic episodes are most often *not* demonic possession, but simply failure of repression. In exploring the lives of psychotic people, one can see a pattern of over-repression which eventually fails, thus resulting in their psychosis.

(6) *Physical illness.* The relationship between mind and body has long been known in medicine. This relationship gave birth to psychosomatic medicine. The effects which the emotions play in physical illness have become increasingly known to the point where some medical authorities estimate that as much as two-thirds of systemic illnesses have emotional conflicts as their partial or total etiology.

Arthritis is one illness which seems closely related to underlying, unresolved anger. Another is cancer. As a medical student in the fifties, I sensed a relationship between the emotions and cancer because of my psychological background. Recent studies have shown that people who typically repress their anger over a period of years do indeed have a greater incidence of cancer than do people who express their anger openly and appropriately at the time of its onset.

Given a condition where one does not express his emotions but represses them into his unconscious, thus containing them like a volatile, smoking time bomb, he might well expect his physical health and general well-being will begin to decline. And so it does. Eventually physical symptoms and significant systemic illnesses develop.

Man does not work in independent sections. He is a whole. Body and soul work together. Our minds affect our emotions, which affect our bodies, which experience sensations to be recorded in our minds, which affect our emotions, which . . . I think you see what I mean.

In particular we have been considering how the mind affects the personality, how it is in fact joined to and works as part of the personality. It's the 'I,' the soul, the person each of us is and is becoming. In this chapter we have discussed how the topology of the mind and how the unconscious part of it affects behavior. We're ready now to look at the reasons why we behave the way we do, and how spiritual growth might be expected to change our behavior.

8

Why Do I Do That?

The glory of this latter house shall be greater than of the former, saith the Lord of hosts: and in this place will I give peace, saith the Lord of hosts. (Haggai 2:9)

Motivators of Behavior

Spiritual growth implies a change in our actions. As we grow, we will act differently toward ourselves and toward God. But the particular evidence of spiritual growth which is most easily seen is how we act toward others.

Change in the way we act implies underlying motives. We have divided the motivations of behavior into categories, to better understand why man acts as he does. We have attempted to make these categories all-inclusive to explain all behavior.

> Motivation by the old sin nature.
> Motivation by memories from childhood.
> Motivation by the unconscious.
> Motivation by the ego.
> Motivation by the conscience (superego).
> Motivation by self-image.
> Motivation by demonic oppression.
> Motivation by indwelling evil spirits.
> Motivation by the Holy Spirit.

Motivation by the Old Sin Nature

There is an aspect of every man which remains an integral part of his biological heritage throughout life. Because he is a slave at birth to this aspect, called man's *old nature,* or *id,* or *the flesh,* man continues to delight in sinning until his salvation. Then, though he is no longer a slave to his *flesh,* his old sin nature continues as a powerful motivator of behavior.

That the flesh is a lifelong irritant comes as a distinct surprise and, I might add, a despair to many Christians. Penned for future generations of believers, the seventh chapter of Romans depicts Paul's frustration in the battle he continually experienced:

> For I delight in the law of God after the inward man:
> But I see another law in my members, warring against the law of my mind, and bringing me into captivity to the law of sin which is in my members. (Rom. 7:22, 23)
>
> For the flesh lustesth against the Spirit, and the Spirit against the flesh: and these are contrary one to the other: so that ye cannot do the thing that ye would . . . .
> Now the works of the flesh are manifest, which are these: Adultery, fornication, uncleanness, lasciviousness,
> Idolatry, witchcraft, hatred, variance, emulations, wrath, strife, seditions, heresies,
> Envyings, murders, drunkenness, revellings, and such like. (Gal. 5:17, 19-21)

The struggle Christians experience is evident in these two passages. Their flesh and their spirits 'war' with one another.

The Scriptures give an answer. We are to "mortify" (Col. 3:5) the deeds of the flesh. Mortifying the flesh is essentially the task of putting to death (or taking away the desire for) the self-serving behavior in one's life. In psychological terms, we move from the pleasure principle—whatever feels good for me regardless of what it does to others, the principle by which children generally operate in their dealings with others—to the maturity of the reality principle, which bases action on delaying self-gratification because of a concern for others' welfare.

Since the old sin nature has operated universally from birth, each person has practiced satisfying it for some time—practiced it to the point of its becoming ingrained. In the eyes of the world, it is the way things should be. Part of the old sin nature is conscious, part unconscious. Everyone is conscious at times of serving himself rather than serving others.

Decisions about which nature we will serve must be made continuously. As an example, let us take the situation of my returning home following a hard day's work. I seat myself comfortably in a leisure chair. Snowball, my faithful old dog, scratches to get in or out. Now comes the decision—will I continue to take my ease, satisfying my needs, or will I attend to his needs?

It is tempting to say, "He has been lying around all day, resting. I deserve to rest now!" On the other hand, since Snowball can't talk, there is no way of knowing whether he desperately needs to heed nature's call or just desires to sniff around a bit. Multiply this decision by hundreds daily and the struggle is placed into magnified perspective. Most thoughtful, introspective believers are constantly aware of this struggle inside them. The old sin nature, seeking to get pleasure, motivates how we act.

Motivation by Memories from Childhood

A second potent category of motivators consists of the memories one carries from earliest life. The old sin nature acts as a motivator of behavior in 'things I would like to do to others'; our memories, on the other hand, act as motivators to seek protection in the present for the actions which have been done to us in the past. As the proverb states, "The burned child dreads the fire!"

Many children have been sexually abused, young girls by some male neighbor or family member; young males, perhaps in a homosexual manner or encounter. Some children lose a significant person, perhaps a parent, to death. Some are fortunate enough to be provided with substitute parental love. For me, it was a beloved maternal grandmother. Other children have been physically abused by natural or stepparents. And if not physically abused, they have been verbally abused so that they become emotionally impotent.

A woman who came to me as a patient was almost wooden in her emotional responses. This woodenness resulted from years of repressed feelings which came from her insensitive and sometimes abusive parents. Once we brought into awareness her deeply repressed anger, she began experiencing "dry heaves," as though her body was saying she could no longer stomach what had happened to her. Under the ministry of the Holy Spirit, her woodenness, like cold wax thawing, began melting.

How many readers were not wanted by their parents, the vessels through whom God chose to give them birth? Or, like Cinderella, saw brothers and sisters receive preferential treatment? Or were constantly denied material goods? And were frustrated in their desire to have individuality with respect, privacy and dignity? Later in life, how many then suffered at the hands of an insensitive spouse or underwent a traumatic divorce? All these events are recorded in the central nervous system in the form of never-to-be-forgotten memories, but perhaps repressed from conscious awareness, as in the case of the lady just mentioned.

In the adult form, memories are two-part recordings in the nervous system. First there is the picture, for which we use the words *ideational recording*. Then there are the feelings, or the *affective recording.* Before the brain has developed the sophistication necessary to record two-part memories, experiences happening to a person are recorded chemically (that is *affectively*) only. There may be just the emotion recorded without the picture, depending on the person's age at the time of the experience.

In computer technology language, a person is programed by his memories. Programed to love by happy memories. Or programed for chronic anger and avoidance of other people by unhappy memories. Perhaps that is the meaning of Prov. 23:7: "For as he thinketh in his heart, so is he." This illustrates the potential power of these bygone memories.

"Train up a child in the way he should go" (Prov. 22:6) has direct application for the memory bank and its later effects on the child. A person whose early memories are mainly happy will be much more friendly and outgoing than a person whose early memories are unhappy. Adults with a paucity of childhood memories are found in therapy to have had emotionally deprived experiences and the unpleasant content of those experiences has been repressed.

For the Christian, Satan's primary point of attack is the mind. I believe that a Christian's spirit is denied to access by Satan because it is sealed at salvation: "In whom also after that ye believed, ye were sealed with that holy Spirit of promise" (Eph. 1:13). Since the body responds to the mind's directions, Satan focuses his forays at the mind.

Satan knows what memories form a part of the memory bank. These can be activated at any given time to motivate behavior. For a person experiencing considerable failure in the past, these memories may cause the person to lessen his Christian efforts. We have heard that success breeds success and failure breeds failure. The 'breeding' is sponsored by memories. In Jeremiah's words, "My soul hath them [the memories of 'mine affliction and my misery'] still in remembrance, and is humbled in me" (Lam. 3:20).

An example of the inhibiting effects of memories came from one of my patients who related a feeling of "apart-ness" even in a crowd, and a feeling of being inadequate because of this awareness. We distinguished between feelings of inadequacy and of exclusion, and she saw that she was merely excluded. As she grappled with this distinction, she concluded that she was not really excluded, either; but she decided that she was the one who excluded others.

"Why are you shutting your psychological gate?" I asked. As a smile spread slowly across her face, she said softly, nodding, "Everyone in the past who was supposed to love me—mother, dad, brother, sister—rejected me. I put up my gate to keep others from getting in and hurting me."

How powerful are memories in their ability to keep us from reaching out and shedding "the love of God . . . abroad in our hearts" (Rom. 5:5)!

As a further example of how memories motivate and affect behavior, a female patient bewailed the spiritual warfare she was experiencing. She and her husband had attended worship services the previous evening, and she felt she had been victorious, but now was feeling extremely anxious again. She had been 'binding Satan' all day, praying intermittently. In exploring the origin of her anxiety, she commented that her husband had called earlier in the day. Following his call, she felt knots in her stomach which indicated intense anxiety.

We focused on her present symptoms in connection with the past. She related an incident from the time when she was eight years old. She was the ring bearer in a relative's wedding. Never having attended a wedding, she was anxious. As everyone left the altar following rehearsal, she felt all alone and began to cry. Her mother looked disgusted and disdainful, and she chided her daughter. As a result, the little girl felt unassured, rejected and abandoned.

She needed her mother's protection and guidance in this situation as well as in many others like it, protection she seldom obtained. She had repressed the desire for her mother's love, but those wishes still struggled for behavioral expression. Therefore, she had transferred these feelings onto her husband. In effect, he became the mother on whom she still overly depended; as he went, so went her feelings—and they were on a seesaw course much of the time.

Unconsciously, she desired him to be strong and loving to compensate for the memories of the mother she never had. It was not spiritual warfare she felt, but merely God allowing some of her repressed conflicts to surface; he could then heal her, showing her how to be independent and emotionally resilient, depending on Him who would never rebuff, disdain nor leave her like both the mother and the husband.

God does this all the time, helping us to change our earliest memories with the balm of His love.

Motivation by the Unconscious

The purpose and function of the unconscious as well as some of the major areas it affects have been described previously. The unconscious develops for our protection. Repression places painful mental content from conscious awareness into the unconscious, where it still has a tremendous impact on behavior. David sensed this impact when he wrote "in the hidden part thou shalt make me to know wisdom" (Ps. 51:6). The unconscious is a normal part of man's mental functioning, but because of its hidden nature, it lends itself to Satan's attacks in Christian lives.

From an early age children have wish-fulfilling, self-serving fantasies which, though repressed, continue motivating behavior throughout life. Children typically want to possess the opposite-sexed parent; little boys want to possess their mothers, little girls their fathers, both for more complete attention and sense of importance.

Some time ago our young son stated candidly, "Dad, I wish you would stay at work and not come home!" To confirm my discernment of his motives I asked why. "Then I could have mama all the time!" he said. He could well have added, "To love me completely and without interruptions from other people." How greedy the old sin nature is! We all repressed this wish into the unconscious, but many of us as adults are motivated in our relationships by the same wish.

Also, our more violent wishes toward siblings or others—"I'd like to kill you!"—often become part of the unconscious. Desire for self-aggrandizing acts such as murder, incest and other sexual immoralities are repressed. So are fantasies of omnipotence, of importance, based on insecurity.

A lawyer, president of a non-denominational businessmen's Christian group chapter, refuses to allow elections despite the bylaw's provisions for mandatory yearly elections. Paradoxically, a lawyer whose training and livelihood are sworn to upholding the law, flagrantly breaks the law as part of his Christian witness. It's safe to say that long-repressed feelings of insecurity with a need for approval, cause him, despite his loving the Lord, to hang on to his office.

Spiritual growth will make a difference in how these old motivations cause people to behave. Some of the old ways, coming from desires repressed into the unconscious, show up in pushing oneself ahead at the expense of others. We also see unresolved anger which erupts towards others periodically, or chronic disappointments and rejections which surface in continual criticism of the efforts of others. All these actions are in marked contrast to the spiritual fruit of love, which comes to fullness as the person grows. Then we see the person acting in a way that is long-suffering, kind, not envious, not easily provoked, trusting and patient.*

Motivation by the Ego

The ego has been discussed in an earlier chapter in conjunction with the old sin nature and the conscience. In its unique position it motivates and directs much behavior. The ego is an organization of mental systems which develops as the mind's go-between for the flesh and external reality, the world. Because the unchanging, old sin nature in the form of man's biological drives always seeks self-gratification, God placed within the personality the capacity for an ego whose purpose is to struggle with the demands of the flesh and to satisfy them in a socially acceptable way. In the Christian, this way also needs to be consistent with God's Word.

The ego is faced with numerous decisions each day; how to meet the needs of hunger, sleep, physical comfort, sexual satisfaction, affection, love, belonging and a host of other needs. In making these decisions, a strong ego makes decisions where the demands of the flesh are met in a reasonable, acceptable manner (Rom. 12:2). A 'weak' ego gives in to the flesh, often making poor choices.

A weak ego is seen where a person has not reckoned himself dead to sin** in some area. Peter depicts the constant struggle which the ego experiences: "Dearly beloved, I beseech you as strangers and pilgrims, abstain from fleshly lusts [id], which war against the soul [ego]" (1 Pet. 2:11). The Christian with a

---

* 1 Cor. 13:4-7
** Romans 6:11

weak ego continues deciding to sin for its gratification rather than deciding to stand fast against the flesh's demands.

We might think of the ego as the executive function of the personality; it has to make judgments, decisions, compromises, evaluations, and solutions by continually sizing up the urgency of an internal need and determining how that need can be met in the outside world. The ego learns to say, "No!" to the old sin nature, supplying a counterbalance to it as a motivator of behavior.

Motivation by the Conscience (Superego)

As a motivator of behavior, the conscience has far-reaching consequences. We have said that the conscience develops out of the ego, that decision-making portion of mental functioning. The conscience sits in judgment on the ego, acting as a referee to determine when acts are 'out of bounds.'

In any given situation, the ego has a wide range of choices for action, some of which the conscience can readily allow as being reasonable; others it frowns on as being unreasonable. The conscience signals the unreasonableness or unacceptability of a course of action by the awareness of guilt, a painful sensation sometimes described as "feeling bad." The awareness of guilt means your conscience is signaling you to change direction; or, if the action is already completed, not to do it again!

As we have seen before, the conscience judges your actions by what it has been taught. The parents are the primary molders of the conscience. What they approve, the person comes to approve; what they disapprove, the person generally disapproves.

We also learned that the conscience is ever on guard, scanning the lists of dos and don'ts for infractions. Woe to the person who steps out of his conscience's lines.

Because the conscience actually represents the parents who are psychologically 'taken inside,' it represents omissions, distortions, and overstrictness presented by the parents, depending on the parent's stability during the child's formative years. I had one patient remark, "It is almost as if my mother sits on my shoulder and tells me not to do something." His statement accurately reflects the origin of the conscience.

The fact that everyone has different parents accounts for the wide differences in strength of conscience. Those people with poorly developed consciences feel relatively little guilt, while persons with overdeveloped consciences—punitive superegos—feel guilt over a wide range of actions. In the latter case, these people may be practically paralyzed to act because of their guilt. Christians with too much conscience are easy to recognize because there are so many things they 'can't do,' for fear of feeling bad. Where the conscience is overdeveloped, it indicates the parents were overly strict and too critical of what the child did. A conscience can thus become an inhibiting motivator.

The conscience can so direct behavior because it functions by inflicting the pain of guilt and denying the self any love. Who likes to be denied love? The "bad" feeling comes from the denial of love to the self.

Although the conscience is an internal device for the purpose of evaluating and censoring behavior, for setting standards and values, often it is manipulated externally by denominational teachings. In fact, it is startling how much behavior is directed by inducing guilt.

For instance, some churches prohibit coed swimming. They segregate by sexes, each to his own chaperoned section. Some denominations have such an inhibiting legalistic foundation that they resemble the Judaizers addressed in Hebrews. The problem was illustrated by Peter: "And there came a voice to him, Rise, Peter; kill, and eat. But Peter said, Not so, Lord; for I have never eaten any thing that is common or unclean" (Acts 10:13, 14). Legalism bound Peter. Others caught in its grip cannot experience their freedom in Christ. They cannot love God for fearing His wrath.

The collective conscience of a group becomes institutionalized in legalistic denominations. "Brother, if you do not witness to ten souls weekly you are in bad shape with the Lord!" (Substitute any other good work for "ten souls.") Believers who are in these denominations may fear the loss of their salvation: therefore they attempt to work their way to heaven.

A good portion of the money dropped in the collection plate is in response to the tenor of the offertory invitation. It sometimes is a demand. Not only does, "What will others think if I do not contribute?" run through many heads; but also they hear, "God sees you, child!" Those who feel angry with God, or who feel delinquent in some way, make offerings to appease their sense of guilt rather than because "God loveth a cheerful [hilarious] giver" (2 Cor. 9:7). So a person may do all the right things for all the wrong reasons.

I have seen many believers who, though Spirit-filled, continue to doubt their salvation. Some even report a spirit of doubt from which they seek deliverance! I "try the spirits" (1 John 4:1) of those who come to me with such a complaint.

The Word states, "For with the heart man believeth unto righteousness; and with the mouth confession is made unto salvation" (Rom. 10:10).

Right! No strings attached. No qualifying clauses. No fine print. No limitations.

"Yes, I did that, but . . . ."

Okay, then, "For God so loved the world, that he gave his only begotten Son, that whosoever believeth in [receiveth] him should not perish, but have everlasting life" (John 3:16).

"I've done that, but . . . ."

As I tried their spirits, my spirit sensed the righteousness of Jesus in them. So what is happening? What blocks their intellectual reception of spiritual rebirth? In my experience, the explanation of the continued doubt has been twofold: either the person is a 'borderline' personality, or the questioning comes from *an unconscious sense of guilt.* Since the latter involves the conscience, let us see how it works.

In relationship terms, salvation is God *accepting* you; not *approving* of you or your actions. The words of the gospel hymn express it: "Just as I am, without one plea, but that Thy blood was shed for me, and that Thou *biddest* me come to Thee!" No changing, no measuring up, just acceptance.

People who have been overly criticized all their lives by domineering parents, and who have not felt acceptance, find it difficult themselves to accept God's unqualified offer. Unconsciously, they have a pervasive sense of guilt over the issue of their basic worthiness. Their questioning is unrelated to God's accepting, even though that is a spiritual fact.* Neither can their feelings decide this issue; feelings are irrelevant. Their questioning is whether their *desirability,* (and in their own eyes, at that) merits acceptance by divine love. Resolving the issue of too much guilt resolves concern over salvation in such cases.

Guilt is used as a controlling device, not only by various denominations, but in daily private social exchanges. Parents control children, spouses control spouses, lovers control lovers, friends control friends, and salesmen control prospective buyers, all through guilt, through being made to feel 'bad' if one does not pursue the desired course of action. Do you, as

---

* Romans 10:9, 10

an adult, visit your parents because you love them or because you feel guilty if you do not? (After all, they may die soon!) Is your church attendance based on guilt? How about a gift to your spouse? Or attendance at PTA? Reflection may startle the reader as to what portion of his behavior is motivated by his conscience when it inflicts the pain of guilt.

Motivation by the Self-Image

A person may display himself publicly in certain ways, and he may behave in certain ways. But his behavior may be at wide variance with his self-image. Self-image is what a person truly thinks of himself.

Often the self-image is not at all the same as another's objective evaluation of him or her. Take the case of a physically striking woman who felt she was ugly. Her self-image was very different from her appearance.

And not long ago I was pleased when a severely disturbed patient wore a red dress, quite in contrast to her usual conservative blues and browns. She said she was beginning to feel pretty. Her self-image was changing to one of greater acceptance of her own needs and desires. Her parents had not allowed her to choose bright colors when she was a child, since the "Lord likes somber colors." With her warm-colored dress, she was accepting her desire to wear bright colors, and thus accepting her own feelings. By accepting her feelings she lessened the distortions of her self-image.

On the other hand, arrogant, prideful people overvaluate themselves; their self-image is also distorted. This overvaluation gives rise to the saying, "If I could buy him for what he is worth and sell him for what he thinks he is worth . . . !"

The more severely disturbed the patient is, the more distorted his self-image is likely to be. Girls with alcoholic fathers suffer from a poor sense of femininity in their self-image. Girls or boys with schizophrenic parents, particularly the mother, routinely suffer from a poorly formed self-image.

Typically, self-image motivates behavior by inhibiting a person's expression of God-given talent for God's glory. How often has God's Kingdom suffered and His glory been robbed by a believer who declines to give his/her services because of self-image! God has given natural gifts to all His children;* to some, beautiful voices; to some, teaching ability; to others, financial acumen; and so on. But haven't you heard the comment, "I'm not good enough," when the statement is based on a poor self-image rather than on objective evaluation?

As Christians, we lead with our best singers, teachers and preachers. And we can, because God has abundantly blessed the Body with talents—that is, if those who possess the talents *will* to use them for Him. Self-image as a motivator so often obstructs expression of these talents. Remaining only latent capacities, they give no glory or praise to the Lord. Nor do they provide the person any real satisfaction.

In motivating behavior, self-image also blocks forgiveness. One of the components of unforgiveness is the feeling of anger. As a defense, anger serves the purpose of keeping people at a psychological distance.

Unforgiveness is the psychological defense which prevents the offending person from reentering your fellowship. I deny the other person fellowship because I fear that, if I let him in, he will wound me again. The self-image is so tenuous in such cases that it cannot stand being hurt again. This unforgiveness continues, and the anger is not released.

Anger, therefore, serves to protect the self-image. In the church family, protecting the self-image prohibits unity of the Body so vital for strength.** Eventually anger, rather than

---

* James 1:17
** Ephesians 4:3

protecting the self-image, may undermine it further.

At any rate, what we think of ourselves has a powerful effect on what we do.

Motivation by Demonic Oppression

Until now the devil has not been mentioned as a prime motivator of behavior. It was necessary first to outline the parts of man's psychological functioning and how these motivate his behavior without Satan's influence. However, Christians "wrestle . . . against principalities, against powers, against the rulers of the darkness of this world, against spiritual wickedness in high places" (Eph. 6:12). Satan is on the prowl because he, "as a roaring lion, walketh about, seeking whom he may devour" (1 Pet. 5:8). But Satan cannot create.* He can only substitute, distort and pervert. God had created the Garden in its perfection before Satan could exert his influence.**

If Satan oppresses us, what part does he act on? He attacks the motivators of behavior natural to man's function, especially when they are working out of balance. Demonic oppression then is satanic influence on the old sin nature.

Satan's oppression is seen in many places in the Scriptures, affecting even the disciples of Jesus. In Mark we read that Jesus told them of His upcoming crucifixion, referring to the Old Testament prophecies.***

> And he spake that saying openly. And Peter took him, and began to rebuke him.
>
> But when he had turned about and looked on his disciples, he rebuked Peter, saying, Get thee behind me, Satan: for thou savourest not the things that be of God, but the things that be of men [of the old sin nature]. (Mark 8:32, 33)

---

* John 1:3
** Gen. 3:4, 5
*** Isa. 53:4, 5

Satan used Peter's desire to have Jesus with him forever as motivation to rebuke Jesus.

A second illustration deals with Ananias and Sapphira. Peter said to them, "Ananias, why hath Satan filled thine heart to lie to the Holy Ghost, and to keep back part of the price of the land" (Acts 5:3). In selling a parcel of land, Ananias had voluntarily agreed to give the entire price to the New Testament church, to impress the people. However, his greed overcame his agreement. Satan must have pointed out how Ananias could have his money and be well thought of, too.

In both of these cases, Satan's intrusive influence worked on already existing motivations in opposition to the moving of the Spirit.

Another interesting incident involves Gehazi, Elisha's servant. Elisha had healed Naaman of leprosy, and Naaman, an influential man, attempted to give Elisha material goods. Elisha declined. Then "Gehazi . . . said, Behold, my master hath spared Naaman this Syrian, in not receiving at his hands that which he brought: but, as the Lord liveth, I will run after him, and take somewhat of him" (2 Kings 5:20). Running ahead to meet Naaman, Gehazi deceived him, receiving silver and garments, a fact which Elisha knew through discernment. Chiding Gehazi, Elisha pronounces, "The leprosy therefore of Naaman shall cleave unto thee, and unto thy seed for ever. And he went out from his presence a leper as white as snow" (2 Kings 5:27). Gehazi allowed his greed to go against the will of God as expressed by His prophet Elisha.

Then there was the case of Isaac's sons. The time came for Isaac to pass his blessing to his eldest son, Esau. Overhearing her husband tell Esau to make preparations for the blessing, Rebekah urged her youngest but favorite son, Jacob, to deceive his father at the risk of his father pronouncing a curse upon him instead of a blessing. Although Jacob was blessed by his father, the deception, sponsored by Satan, caused a family rift lasting for some years.*

As the god of this world,** Satan has power; nevertheless, it is limited. God says, "Greater is he that is in you [Christian believers], than he that is in the world" (1 John 4:4). God placed Satan's power in perspective when the prophet Isaiah wrote "I have created the waster to destroy" (Isa. 54:16). Destroy what? Jesus threw light on this issue: "If any man will come after me, let him deny himself, and take up his cross, and follow me" (Matt. 16:24). Denying 'self' refers to fleshly desires. In this sense it might be said that Satan helps us to deny our flesh, our motivators from the id.

Satan? Our response to that idea is: "But I thought Satan was battling believers instead of helping them!" But suppose we ask the question, how does one correct a weakness in any system?

We correct weakness first of all by detection. In sports, a typical strategy is to attack the weakest spot in the defense until it is strengthened. In professional football, a rookie cornerback is often the prime focus of the opposing team's passing attack. In this light we begin to see the usefulness of Satan in God's scheme of moving the world toward restoration of holiness. Not long ago, God spoke to my spirit, recalling my childhood in South Carolina. There, the gnats in summer seemed intolerable. They had a peculiar sweet taste when they flew into your mouth. God reminded me that, pesky as they seemed, gnats in the house pointed to an area that needed a new screen.

In the same way, the child of God is under God's protection.*** You are already 'screened' but God uses Satan to point out areas where refurbished spiritual screens are needed. In oppression, Satan may work by deception.**** He

---
* Gen. 27:1-46
** 2 Cor. 4:4
*** James 4:8
**** Gen. 3:4

may discourage. He may tempt by perverting natural desires. Nevertheless, oppression is a marker which indicates an area that needs change.

If you are oppressed by depression God is showing you how your emotions are being handled incorrectly.* If you are oppressed by thoughts that something will happen to your children, God is showing a need for greater emotional separation.** If you are oppressed by financial needs, God may be indicating a need for better stewardship.*** Suppose you are oppressed by envy and jealousy over the neighbor's new Cadillac. Through Satan's oppression, God is indicting a need in self-image change.**** While there are many other areas which could be mentioned, these are representative of areas where Christians often experience oppression.

Oppression should be the occasion for taking stock, to see whether we are being "conformed to the image of his Son" (Rom. 8:29). In the hands of God Satan becomes a flesh-scraping tool. We become aware of sore places, of what needs to be healed or changed.

Satan cannot oppress anything that is not there, any more than a middle-C tuning fork can cause the middle-C piano string to vibrate if it is lacking. In other words, Satan can only focus on psychological weaknesses. As the appropriate changes are made, Satan's oppression in the formerly weak areas must diminish and cease. It's rather like plugging a leaking dam. After a number of failures, one may hear an accusing voice that says, "See, you will never make it!" That only spurs more effort, and redoubled efforts *will* repair and strengthen the dam. Stan perverts man's desires to attain his ends, discouraging the believer through deception, but the committed Christian perseveres in the face of the devil's efforts.

We should say here that all desires are not improper. Desire

---

* Eph. 4:26
** Luke 9:62
*** Matt. 25:21
**** Phil. 4:6, 7

to know Christ,* desire for Christians to grow spiritually** and desire for salvation of heathen*** are all commendable. God has given man many desires, some of them sexual, physical, and mental, which may be appropriately satisfied by exercising or pursuing them in moderation. However, Satan attempts to cause immoderation in various areas of our lives, such as gluttony (too much eating); sexual immorality (sex under inappropriate circumstances); and idolatry (pursuit of anything to the point of worship).

Oppression is the only *external* category of motivators; all others are internal. This fact emphasizes the need to change all other motivators insofar as possible, strengthening them, and protecting against immoderate desires in other areas.

Motivation by Indwelling Evil Spirits

Indwelling evil spirits may be taken by some people to mean demon possession; however, I personally do not believe Christians can be demon-possessed. I use the term "indwelling evil spirits" in a somewhat different way. But first let us look at a scriptural passage that is used by some to contest that believers cannot have evil spirits inside themselves. It is:

> Know ye not that your body is the temple of the Holy Ghost which is in you, which ye have of God, and ye are not your own?
>
> For ye are bought with a price: therefore glorify God in your body, and in your spirit, which are God's. (1 Cor. 6:19, 20)

This passage is used to say that salvation excludes believers from demon possession. But is this true, without reservation? Does salvation bring *automatic* exclusion from evil spirits?

Jesus commented, "If ye *continue* in my word, then ye are

---
* Phil. 3:10
** Gal. 4:19
*** Romans 10:1

my disciples indeed; And ye shall know the truth, and the truth shall make you free" (John 8:31, italics added). We are cautioned "to *continue* in the grace of God" (Acts 13:43), to *"continue* in the faith . . . of God" (Acts 14:22), and "to *continue* in prayer" (Col. 4:2). Jesus said also, "If ye abide [continuously] in me, and my words abide in you, ye shall ask what ye will, and it shall be done unto you" (John 15:7). To persevere, to continue, gives protection in "work[ing] out your own salvation with fear and trembling," (Phil. 2:12). Continuing in the Word, in the grace of God and in prayer, all part of abiding in Christ, provides an excluding factor with regard to evil spirits.

In the same way that well-constructed and properly maintained residential dwellings provide protection against natural elements, so will a well-maintained spiritual temple provide protection against spiritual elements. However, in the same way that poorly maintained dwellings allow entrance to rats and roaches as well as to natural elements, a poorly maintained spiritual temple will eventually provide access to evil spirits. And when we look about the Body, we can see temples in various states of disrepair!

Jesus gave members of the Body, His Church, effective power against indwelling evil spirits. In His last-recorded words before He ascended, He said, "In my name shall they cast out devils" (Mark 16:17). The effects of these indwelling, restricting demons is seen in the Gadarene demoniac:

> But when he saw Jesus afar off, he ran and *worshipped him,*
>
> And cried with a loud voice, and said, What have I to do with thee, Jesus, thou Son of the most high God? I adjure thee by God, that thou torment me not.
>
> For he said unto him, Come out of the man, thou unclean spirit. (Mark 5:6-8, italics added)

Even in the man's condition, he worshiped Jesus! And when he had been delivered of the legion of evil spirits, he sat with Jesus, clothed and in his right mind.

But one must be very careful not to mistakenly attribute indwelling spirits for all aberrant behavior. Jesus laid the basis for a differential diagnosis in cases of sickness:

> And his fame went throughout all Syria: and they brought unto him all sick people that were taken with [1] divers diseases and [2] torments, and those which were [3] possessed with devils, and those which were [4] lunatick, and those that had the [5] palsy; and he healed them. (Matt. 4:24)

As we can see, only one condition in this group is demon possession. Not only here, but in no less than seventeen Scripture verses in the original manuscripts, a distinction is made between illnesses from a demonic cause (*daimonidzemenous*) and sickness from natural causes (*kakos* or *astenos*).*

In addition to the scriptural evidence, I have personal, clinical evidence for my position. I have prayed successful deliverance over many Christians, including Spirit-filled believers. In these cases, the ensuing behavior change was unrelated to any placebo effect, desire to please me, mental set, suggestion, or hysterical phenomenon, each of which would be hard to sustain for any lengthy time. On two occasions while praying for deliverance, the serpentine spirit hissed as it exited, a rather unnerving experience! Therefore, I believe that both the Scriptures and clinical experience support my belief that Christians can 'have' demons.

But how do the evil spirits motivate behavior, and what is the result of successful deliverance? Rather than use the word "demon-possessed," it makes more practical sense to me to visualize demonic invasion as involving isolated sectors of a

---

* Matthew 4:24; 8:16; 10:1, 8; Mark 1:32-34; 3:10, 11; 6:13; 16:17-18; Luke 4:40, 41; 6:18, 19; 7:21; 8:2; 9:1; 13:32; Acts 5:16; 8:7, 8; 19:11, 12

person's life. Evil spirits may affect bits of behavior or attitudes in specific situations. For example, a person may have a spirit of rejection which affects his relationships to the extent that he frequently feels rejected and acts accordingly. In another case, the person may have a spirit of anger which causes frequent loud, intense, prolonged angry behavior. Therefore, evil spirits may be in a Christian to the extent that certain facets of his personality will be affected in a repeated, typical way over which the person cannot seem to get control, either by confession of his fleshly desires or by his will to overcome them.

In my experience, some evil spirits have been in the person at the time of salvation. They entered before salvation. But others came into a person following salvation, probably because of his lack of persevering with the Lord. In fact, continuing in certain types of unscriptural behavior will provide access routes for evil spirits. So also will hurtful memories from earlier times.

Once a person has an evil spirit, that aspect of his behavior becomes "locked in" and he has little choice but to become jealous, angry, or whatever the case may be. Once delivered, he may then have the freedom to practice other behavioral responses in that area of his life. Deliverance does not automatically lead to successful behavior in the specific area; the believer has to practice his new behavioral freedom to perfect it into appropriate social skills.

Motivation by the Spirit

We have considered categories of behavioral motivators in their order from the lowest, the old sin nature, now to the highest, the spirit. Between these extremes have been placed categories as they have exerted a developmental influence—

memories, conscience, ego, unconscious, and self-image—as well as pressures from the adversary. These come in two forms. Satan exerts external influence, or oppression. Or he can affect people internally, through evil spirits which restrict behavioral flexibility in a given sector of one's life. Now last in our discussion we will look at the spirit as a motivator of human behavior, since this part of human functioning has the Holy Spirit as its interface.

The goal of Christian living is walking in the Spirit: "For as many as are led by the Spirit of God, they are the sons of God" (Rom. 8:14). Along this line, the development of, and satisfaction in, any relationship depends on the sensitivity of the partners involved. Spouses, mother/child, or virtually any relationship is marked by increasing sensitivity of each member to the other, if the relationship deepens in significance and satisfaction. God is, of course, sensitive to us, and He intends that we should be sensitive to Him.

Jesus touches on this sensitivity in speaking to His bride: "He that hath an ear, let him hear what the Spirit saith unto the churches" (Rev. 2:29; 3:6; 3:22). This theme is repeated in John: "My sheep hear my voice, and I know them, and they follow me" (John 10:27). First comes sensitivity, then recognition, then obedience.

How wonderful it is to hear the voice of the Great Shepherd and to want to follow in His footsteps! When James says we are "a kind of firstfruits of his creatures" (James 1:18), he urges each believer to "be swift to hear" (1:19). Following salvation, our spiritual ears should become more attuned to heavenly things.

When one begins to hear that beautiful Voice, he responds by availability. Our availability is necessary to propagate the kingdom, for:

> How then shall they call on him in whom they have not believed? and how shall they believe in him of whom they have not heard? and how shall they hear without a preacher?
>
> And how shall they preach, except they be sent? (Rom. 10:14, 15)

And, we might add, how shall they be sent unless they are available?

Jesus provided the model for us, at the age of twelve in the Temple, after the Feast of the Passover. On their way home, Mary and Joseph feared that Jesus was lost. Turning back, they found Him at the feet of the teachers. In response to his mother's chiding, He said, "How is it that ye sought me? wist [knew] ye not that I must be about my Father's business?" (Luke 2:49). Even as a child, Jesus made himself available to God's will. Later he said, "My meat is to do the will of him that sent me" (John 4:34). We gain in strength every time we obey God, just as eating natural food gives strength to our physical bodies.

It has been true throughout the history of God's dealing with His people: "To obey is better than sacrifice" (1 Sam. 15:22). Sacrificing runs the risk of giving what we want to keep for ourselves. Obeying means to commit ourselves completely. God says "[Listen to and] obey my voice, and I will be your God, and ye shall be my people: and walk ye in all the ways that I have commanded you, that it may be well unto you" (Jer. 7:23).

The power which the apostles marveled over in the New Testament church came through their obedience. We define obedience as a psychological functioning, an act or attitude of the soul, for spiritual purposes. Peter knew this when he and the other apostles were commanded by their rulers not to speak any more in the name of Jesus. He told the Sadducees: "We ought to [must] obey God rather than men" (Acts 5:29). The scenario is unchanged since those days; if anything, it has become more urgent: WE MUST OBEY GOD RATHER THAN MEN in these last days.

Without spiritual purpose, man lives only to propagate himself. In so doing he wants only to gratify his own drives. But the Christian believer gets his motivation from the Holy Spirit. Our next chapter tells how this motivator of behavior directs spiritual growth.

9

How We Grow Spiritually

Who hath directed the Spirit of the Lord, or being his counseller hath taught him?

With whom he took counsel, and who instructed him, and taught him in the path of judgment, and taught him knowledge, and shewed to him the way of understanding? (Isa. 40:13, 14)

Spiritual Growth: Its Means

Men do not direct God, or teach Him. Instead we are instructed by Him. We can be taught in the path of judgment, and learn knowledge, and be shown the way of understanding. In order to grow spiritually, Christians must be taught by God. They must become disciples.

The word "Christian" has two meanings. First, it means "of the anointed one," or "of the Christ." Second, it means a disciple, one who learns from God.

The anointing which converts a wicked, deceitful heart, turning it to God, comes only from above, from the mercy of God. It changes a person to one which hungers for ever-closer union with the Father. Once one becomes a Christian, anointed through God's love, the motivation for becoming a disciple comes from within each person.

Sadly, most Christians opt not to become disciples. Discipleship implies a growth/learning process whose purpose is fruit bearing. "Herein is my Father glorified, that ye bear much fruit: so shall ye be my disciples" (John 15:8). Through discipleship one matures enough to bear fruit for the Master.

It's necessary to grow before we can bear fruit. This is illustrated by comparing a new convert to a newly inducted Army recruit. The day years ago when I was sworn in as a raw private, I was as complete with regard to opportunities, privileges, and responsibilities as I would be upon discharge two years later. But, what a raw recruit I was! I needed teaching and molding, transforming into some semblance of a soldier, not only in outward appearance but also in knowledge of, and loyalty to, the service.

Similarly, at the time of salvation the 'babe' is "complete in him [Christ]" (Col. 2:10). Before maturity the Lord has "perfected for ever them that are sanctified" (Heb. 10:14)! Already, the new Christian is "meet to be partakers of the inheritance of the saints in light" (Col. 1:12).

On an experiential basis, however, on a day-to-day basis, the process is just begun. Spiritual basic training must begin in earnest to transform the new believer into one who, like Paul, can say, "I know whom I have believed" (2 Tim 1:12). He becomes one who not only knows but trusts in, and progressively acts on, what he knows about that Person. Woe to the new believer who sees no necessity for continuous basic training to perfect Christian living, for he becomes prey to the adversary, "seeking whom he may devour" (1 Pet. 5:8); under those conditions vigilance and perseverance are imperative.

Each believer has two sides, a divine side and a human side, two differing natures within himself. Therefore, two agents, God and the believer, are involved in spiritual growth. The crux of the issue for a believer is in striking the proper balance between the two aspects. This is a balance which will give God the glory for things He has done while not excluding the believer's responsibility.

We must recognize that God furnishes the energy for growth. Only our abiding dependence on Him provides the relationship undergirding this growth. Despite arrogant pretensions to deny this life-giving and life-sustaining dependence, we must admit that "None can keep alive his own soul" (Ps. 22:29). Though humbling, God's Word provides clear understanding of the source of growth:

"Without me ye can do nothing" (John 15:5).
"Thou also hath wrought all our works in us" (Isa. 26:12).
"Thy God hath commanded thy strength" (Ps. 68:28).
"From me [God] is thy fruit found" (Hos. 14:8).

God places at His children's disposal the necessary means for this growth. The Christian's job is to 'lay aside' the things which hinder, because he wants to grow.*

The Christian's motivation for living comes from the Spirit of God. Channeled through man's spirit, the Holy Spirit directs his soul. In fact, the Holy Spirit directing the soul equals spirit. This is what gives us new life when we accept Christ. Our spirits 'come alive' because God has breathed His Spirit into them. Then His Spirit directs, or motivates, the soul in bearing fruit.

Growth is not instantaneous. Growth is a change in the believer's capacities, and it differs from the works the Holy Spirit does in a believer's life. For instance a patient, following salvation, was enabled to stop smoking, after years of trying unsuccessfully on his own. As a work in this man's life, the Holy Spirit permanently removed his desire for nicotine.

Though relieved of smoking, this believer entered therapy because of an uncontrollable jealousy toward his wife, fearing she would leave him for another man despite her having lived with him comfortably for some twenty years! While he deeply appreciated his newly given nicotine-abstaining ability, the

---
* 1 Peter 2:1, 2

jealousy made him miserable. It threatened his marriage. One evil was taken care of, only to uncover another. The man would continue to be challenged to grow.

Instant change is not according to God's plan for us. "He maketh me lie down in green pastures" (Ps. 23:2) says not so much that God makes things pleasant for us as that He desires *continued* dependence upon Him: it is a proven fact that the need to receive from God increases dependence upon Him. Were He, through grace, to create instant growth in the believer, untold Christians would drift away from that essential bonding with the Shepherd.

The case against instant, unitary change is backed up by the verse, "tribulation worketh patience" (Rom. 5:3). Instant change would deprive us of opportunities to develop patience, a fruit of the Spirit. Therefore, we are commanded to be "rejoicing in hope; patient in tribulation" (Rom. 12:12). Since it is the Father who comforts us in all our tribulations* we learn His love during the trying times. Moreover, through the process of being comforted, we learn to comfort others.

Adults who were not often comforted and snuggled by their parents as children are awkward in snuggling their own children; they have few skills in this area. Slow spiritual growth allows God the time to comfort again and again, establishing a pattern. This comforting can then be passed to others in ministry to them.

Human nature is such that, unless one waits and plans for something desired, he doesn't really appreciate it. You can see this principle when people become suspicious of the quality of bargain goods. If we pay more for them, they must be better. Because of this kind of thinking, slow growth, waiting to attain maturity and experiencing his comfort along the way, promotes a thankful heart toward the Father.

---

* 2 Cor. 1:4

Dependence on the Father and His mercy also tests our faith. Army basic training, simulating actual combat, prepares one to depend on his ability to operate his military weapons when the trust test comes. Depending on the Father, on the spiritual weapons He provides and on His faithfulness, is crucial to success in spiritual warfare.* How much better to learn confidence in His reliability, His grace, His long-suffering, His desire to minister to His children, than to be placed in situations where one *must* turn to God.

Remember, it is God who orders growth-promoting circumstances in our lives. Success in dealing with them depends on a person's perspective; we can view them as obstacles or as steppingstones. If we think of them as obstacles, we grumble. They are interruptions, aggravations and worse. But viewed as steppingstones, the same circumstances become opportunities for 'going up a little higher.' Only through continuous practice do we truly integrate the lessons that become part of our behavior toward others.

Another reason why a person does not change all aspects of his life at one time and grow in every area at once is the fact of individual responsibility. Having ministered many times as a speaker to various groups, I have had opportunities for praying with people under varying circumstances. Many ask God for prayer requests which fall under the area of their own responsibility. The believer must himself assume responsibility for resolving the problem. Of course God provides the means and the information necessary to take constructive steps.

A recurring example in my practice is depression. Many times I have been asked to pray for God to remove depression, an area where most, if not all, responsibility for resolution resides in the believer. Enough is understood, enough is written about this condition, to know that depression occurs through a

---

* Eph. 6:12-18

sequence of events which could be said to constitute unwritten emotional laws.

Many aspects of this world operate in a similar fashion. God is a God of order, of laws. Obeyed and followed, one can minimize many difficulties. Disobeyed, one can predict trouble: "For whatsoever a man soweth, that shall he also reap" (Gal. 6:7). There are dietary laws, economic laws, physiological laws, emotional laws, spiritual laws.

God does not miraculously lift depression, but He does shed the light of His Spirit on it. Once we understand how we have become depressed, He gives us the grace to rectify matters and to produce the spiritual fruit of joy.

"Be ye not unequally yoked" is another example of God's law, yet we see Christians continually marrying nonbelievers. A chaotic marriage most often results. In those cases, when trouble begins, one should not cry out that God is not doing anything. Running one's life according to God's laws and staying within their boundaries makes for success, because God says so. Straying invites the eventual danger of failure, bankruptcy, physical symptoms, or a life of marital drudgery.

The believer's responsibility lies in being willing to learn. He can equip himself with the knowledge necessary for efficiency in every area of his life. With few exceptions, perhaps when he lives in a very isolated area, the believer can obtain information through TV, radio, cassette tapes, books, seminars, correspondence courses. Failure to do so may be considered slothfulness. The believer should not blame God when he himself is at fault for problems about which he could learn and help himself.

In addition to depression, other examples of not doing our homework include misuse of dietary laws by eating improperly or too much (gluttony); and misuse of economic laws, causing severe financial problems. The necessity for earning a living and doing daily household chores demands time and energy. The remaining time, however, may well be spent in pursuit of knowledge which, applied through God's means and direction, yields results in efficient and righteous living.

We have talked about our responsibility in providing the means for spiritual growth. We must yield ourselves, becoming disciples of our Lord Jesus Christ. Then, even as salvation is "the gift of God: not of works, lest any man should boast. For we are His workmanship, created in Christ Jesus unto good works" (Eph. 2:8-10), so is the continuation of that workmanship beyond salvation fashioned by the Holy Spirit. God discharges His responsibility for our spiritual growth through the Holy Spirit.

In Peter's words, "Grace unto you, and peace, be multiplied" (1 Pet. 1:2). When grace is multiplied, Christians grow. This dispenser of grace is the inimitable, limitless Holy Spirit, the Maintainer of the Church age.

Jesus called the Holy Spirit a *Comforter:*

> And I will pray the Father, and he shall give you another Comforter, that he may abide with you for ever. (John 14:16)
>
> Nevertheless I tell you the truth; It is expedient for you that I go away: for if I go not away, the Comforter will not come unto you; but if I depart, I will send him unto you . . . .
>
> Howbeit when he, the Spirit of truth, is come, he will guide you into all truth. (John 16:7, 13)

Dwelling within each believer, that selfsame Holy Spirit guides and directs growth.

Yet this direction, this grace, comes not at the request or the demand of the believer. He divides "to every man severally *as He will*" (1 Cor. 12:11, italics added). As the ever-present

Servant, the Holy Spirit at all times knows what is best for each individual. As His children we implore God for many things in prayer, but the things we desire may be out of sequence. Perhaps we want them too soon for us to handle successfully. Or God may not grant them for reasons known only to Him. The lack of bestowal is not due to any lack of love or concern on God's part; indeed denial may be related to His ultimate concern.

My seven-year-old son makes many requests of me. I consider all of them. But I deny some *because of* my love rather than my lack of love. I know his fancies outweigh his realistic abilities, but there will come a time when he will be able to handle many of the things he fancies now.

The means by which the Spirit dispenses this grace are individual. It is for one person, at one time, and gives the ability to overcome a trial. As Jesus told Paul, "My grace is sufficient for thee: for my strength is made perfect in weakness" (2 Cor. 12:9). Thus, little by little, we develop our overcoming ability through the grace of God.

As Paul said, "I have planted, Apollos watered; but God gave the increase" (1 Cor. 3:6). This overcoming ability, this "increase," in a Christian's life may be better tolerance of pain, or increased patience, or better control of anger, or whatever is needed at the moment. It might also be humility, to reduce pride; or tolerance and acceptance of another's transgressions.

Or the increase which God gives could be the assertiveness to state an opinion, or to witness for Christ. Or it may be strength to love beyond hurt, to minister beyond a sense of personal wounding. Whatever its nature, God dispenses His grace according to His sovereign determination.

Even our concern, our God-directedness, is Holy Spirit-induced, "Not that we are sufficient of ourselves, to think any thing as of ourselves; but our sufficiency is of God" (2 Cor. 3:5). The only good thing in us is the righteousness of Jesus, stirred up anew and replenished daily by the Holy Spirit. Only when one is completely convinced of that statement is he able to yield before God, yield to the degree that he can be "led by the Spirit" (Rom. 8:14). Were it otherwise, the Psalmist would not assert, "He *maketh* me to lie down in green pastures" (Ps. 23:2). The Holy Spirit makes possible all that we do in our growing.

At the outset, Jesus promises this enabling: "Follow me, and *I will make you* fishers of men" (Matt. 4:19, italics added). Notice the order of responsibility and response: Believer first (you "follow me"), God second ("I will make you"). We also see this theme of help by the Holy Spirit for man's limitations in:

> Likewise the Spirit also helpeth our infirmities: for we know not what we should pray for as we ought: but the Spirit itself maketh intercession for us with groanings which cannot be uttered. (Rom. 8:26)

We pray; the Holy Spirit helps us to pray. We move toward Him; it is He who "maketh my way perfect [complete]" (Ps. 18:32). We listen; "He hath done all things well: He maketh both the deaf to hear, and the dumb to speak" (Mark 7:37). As He did physically for the deaf and dumb man, God takes a person who does not 'hear' spiritual direction and makes him to both hear and speak. He promises all these things and more.

God repeatedly invites believers to partake of His enabling power. He says we may "come boldly [intimately, not arrogantly] unto the throne of grace, that we may obtain mercy, and find grace to help in time of need" (Heb. 4:16). In the gospels, He implores:

> Ask, and it shall be given you; seek, and ye shall find; knock, and it shall be opened unto you:
>
> For every one that asketh receiveth; and he that seeketh findeth; and to him that knocketh it shall be opened. (Matt. 7:7, 8)

Moreover, He tells us that "ye have not, because ye ask not" (James 4:2). God wants us to get our help from Him. He's ready to give it.

Many of the children He indwells are not aware of the Holy Spirit as a person. But each one's life depends on Him, beginning when all life came to be through Him. And once the gift of life is bestowed, whether in nature or as human life, it is maintained by the Holy Spirit.

Considering nature alone, the Holy Spirit controls all nature. It is He who tells the pigeons the correct direction in homing toward their base. It is He who tells geese in flight how to assume their pattern as they fly gracefully toward new seasonal homes. It is He who programs the communicational patterns of ants and bees. His operation in this area can best be summarized in Paul's 'Unknown God' oration on Mars Hill:

> God that made the world and all things therein, seeing that he is Lord of heaven and earth, dwelleth not in temples made with hands;
>
> Neither is worshipped with men's hands, as though he needed any thing, seeing he giveth to all life, and breath, and all things. (Acts 17:24, 25)

God made and keeps the universe in order. And He maintains every function of man. Though man has been given a brain to guide regulatory processes in his body, the Holy Spirit is the brain's Regulator; the physiological processes of digestion, circulation, hormones—all owe their finely tuned synchronization to Him in such an intimate way that one can truly say, "For in him we live, and move, and have our being" (Acts 17:28).

God also clearly designated man to have "dominion over the fish of the sea, and over the fowl of the air, and over the cattle, and over all the earth, and over every creeping thing that creepeth upon the earth" (Gen. 1:26). Yet it is only through the internal, unseen working of the Holy Spirit that man is able to maintain this superiority and dominance.

To many believers, the Holy Spirit is impersonal, some*thing* which acts in some vague way to benefit his life. He never becomes *personal,* a person with whom to enjoy an intimate relationship. But the more personal the Holy Spirit becomes, the more satisfying one's spiritual life becomes. He is a person and should be responded to as a person, should be accorded a personal relationship.*

A personal pronoun is used in referring to the Holy Spirit: "And when *he* is come, *he* will reprove the world of sin, and of righteousness, and of judgment" (John 16:8). And as a person, He has the attributes of a person. Let's look at these:

(1) *Intellect:* "But God hath revealed them unto us by his Spirit: for the Spirit searcheth all things, yea, the deep things of God" (1 Cor. 2:10).

(2) *Sensibility or feelings:* "Now I beseech you, brethren, for the Lord Jesus Christ's sake, and for the love of the Spirit, that ye strive together with me in your prayers to God for me" (Rom. 15:30).

(3) *Will:* "And he that searcheth the hearts knoweth what is the *mind* of the Spirit, because he maketh intercession for the saints according to the *will* of God" (Rom. 8:27). The Holy Spirit has intellect, feelings, and will, the attributes of a person.

Furthermore, He must be treated with respect and tenderness,

---

* Riggs, 1949

because the Scriptures say, "Quench not the Spirit" (1 Thess. 5:19). Once quenched, He does not perform the personal acts in the believer's life as quickly as before. Still He works to perform His transformations: "But all these worketh that one and the selfsame Spirit, dividing to every man severally as he will"(1 Cor. 12:11). He teaches: "He shall teach you all things" (John 14:26). He searches: "The Spirit searcheth all things, yea, the deep things of God" (1 Cor. 2:10). He speaks: "As they ministered to the Lord, and fasted, the Holy Ghost said, Separate me Barnabas and Saul for the work whereunto I have called them"(Acts 13:2). He reproves: "And when he is come, he will reprove the world of sin" (John 16:8). He prays: "The Spirit itself maketh intercession for us with groanings which cannot be uttered"(Rom. 8:26). He calls man into service,* and directs men in service.**

The Word tells us much more about the Spirit. The Holy Spirit is related with the other members of the triune Godhead in a personal relationship: "Go ye therefore, and teach all nations, baptizing them in the name of the Father, and of the Son, and of the Holy Ghost" (Matt. 28:19). And throughout history He has interacted with human personalities. About Samson the Bible says, "And the Spirit of the Lord came mightily upon him" (Judges 14:6). A thousand years later the Spirit interacted with Stephen and in his being chosen as one of those who served the widows: "Look ye out among you seven men of honest report, full of the Holy Ghost and wisdom" (Acts 6:3). The Holy Spirit directed Philip's path for ministry when he said, "Go near, and join thyself to this chariot"(Acts 8:29).

The Holy Spirit functions in the lives of contemporary Christians as He did in the lives of those in bygone days to fill their lives and direct their works. He is limited in this desire

---

* Acts 13:2
** Acts 16:6, 7

only by the believer's lack of yielding to His direction. Stubbornness, rebellious attitudes, indifference, self-sufficiency, and carnality form barriers which impede His work. In fulfillment of prophecy, the Holy Spirit longs to fill the believer who wants His infilling: "And be not drunk with wine, wherein is excess; but be filled with the Spirit" (Eph. 5:18). We can each be filled, and live in the joy of that filling.

God promises that He will pour out His Spirit on men. "And it shall come to pass afterward, that I will pour out my spirit upon all flesh" (Joel 2:28). That outpouring is seen in ever-increasing waves in these last days, to impower and transform the believer's life.

Our spiritual growth is made possible when we yield to the Holy Spirit. We may yield to Him because He has first touched us. We may yield when we study His Word and learn His will for us. We may yield when He allows us to go through trials. In every case, we take our sustenance from Him. Ultimately, our spiritual growth depends on the Holy Spirit of God.

10

Why and Where We Grow

The word which came to Jeremiah from the Lord, saying,

Arise, and go down to the potter's house, and there I will cause thee to hear my words.

Then I went down to the potter's house, and, behold, he wrought a work on the wheels.

And the vessel that he made of clay was marred in the hand of the potter: so he made it again another vessel, as seemed good to the potter to make it. (Jer. 18:1-4)

Spiritual Growth: Its Explanation

God, by His Holy Spirit, causes us to grow, just as the potter shaped and reshaped the vessel while Jeremiah watched.

The basis of spiritual growth, the Holy Spirit, works now, during our Church age. For the sinner, He reproves the "world of sin, and of righteousness, and of judgment" (John 16:8), reveals God's "grace" to him (Titus 2:11), urges him to be "saved" (John 6:44), and draws him "to Christ for salvation" (Eph. 2:5). Then for the saint, the Holy Spirit desires to produce fruit in his life, to direct his work and fill his life. Therefore, an essential part of His work during the Church age is the spiritual growth in every believer, as the believer allows.

If the Holy Spirit is the basis, what are the mechanics? We have analyzed this growth and broken it down into its various components which have been outlined in previous chapters.

Such analysis can be helpful for the individual who experiences continual blocking in any area of his life. Perhaps you, or other believers you know, have agonized in prayer over particular sins, seemingly without success. Although saved and Spirit-filled, victory eludes you again and again. You are doing all you *know* to do, but as yet you have no "song in the night" (Ps. 77:6).

In this chapter we will look at specific ways through which the Holy Spirit works in lives to sponsor spiritual growth. This working is like the motor which provides energy for a car. Suppose we could specify the engine's parts and tell how any of them might need adjustment. We would then provide information which, if used, could lead to more efficient performance because the parts would be working together more harmoniously for the purpose for which they were made. So it is also with the Holy Spirit. It provides the energy, the gasoline. And when the different parts of the personality work well together, spiritual growth happens. As with the car we can say, "Now we're getting somewhere."

The depth of the Holy Spirit's power to effect these changes is expressed very clearly in the following passage from the Scriptures:

> And what is the exceeding greatness of his power to us-ward who believe, according to the working of his mighty power,
>
> Which he wrought in Christ, when he raised him from the dead, and set him at his own right hand in the heavenly places,
>
> Far above all principality, and power, and might, and dominion, and every name that is named. (Eph. 1:19-21)

The same power which raised Jesus from the dead is the

power residing in each believer to accomplish those spiritual changes.

Before proceeding to an extended discussion of these various areas of change, we list five general principles which we believe determine growth:

(1) Growth occurs: (a) over time with, (b) change in size, (c) differentiation in structure, (d) change in form, and (e) in sequential progression.

(2) In sponsoring spiritual growth, the Holy Spirit works to modify existing psychological structures and functions rather than creating new ones.

(3) Spiritual growth recapitulates psychosexual development.

(4) Spiritual growth can develop no further than one's psychosexual growth or development.

(5) The believer may play a facilitative or an obstructive role in his spiritual growth.

Some purists may object that, since man is different from plants and animals, his spiritual growth occurs in response to different laws from those governing his physical growth. But I see God as an economical God, who set up all processes to work under one grand design. For instance, He is a God of time, as any believer impatient for change in some area of his life will agree. Growth then occurs over time, with changes in size, structures and form, in an orderly progression. Whoever heard of a rose appearing before the stem and thorns? Or a person becoming a fully developed adult at the age of two? All nature appears to be governed by this first principle of growth.

Therefore, spiritual growth occurs step-by-step, modifying existing psychological structures. It is the second principle of progress towards maturity. The third principle above, however, may stir objections. I believe that spiritual growth recapitulates (reviews and summarizes again) psychosexual development. As an example, we observe that the first lesson learned in the relationship with God is trust, the same first lesson learned with the parents by the infant. As we have pointed out, that lesson may be only incompletely learned by either the infant or the 'babe in Christ.' We have seen other parallels in spiritual and psychosexual growth in chapter three.

Objections might also be raised to the statement that one cannot advance further in his spiritual growth than he has in his psychosexual development. But observations of three groups—adolescents who receive salvation, middle-aged adults who were saved in the middle age, and middle-aged adults who were saved as young adults—gave evidence consistent with this principle. For instance, when motives are considered, service for the Lord may be placed in clearer perspective: much of one's activity for the Lord may be done to avoid the spouse, to avoid guilt, to receive approval, to get self-gratification or to feel important. Since God looks on the heart,* He knows to what extent Christian service is not based on love for Him! So from the vantage point of countless hours of clinical experience with Christians, and in teaching ministry and social interactions with the three groups above, we have concluded that one's spiritual growth does not extend beyond his level of psychosexual development.

If a person has been rebellious with his parents and other authorities, he will be rebellious with God. If he never learned to trust his parents and others, he continues experiencing doubts about God's reliability and goodness. If the person never outgrew his dependence and manifests behavior symptomatic of his unresolved dependency, such as by the use of drugs or alcohol, he will experience the same problems in his relationship with the Lord.

---

* 1 Sam. 16:7

John, the beloved disciple, lends scriptural support to this conclusion when he says,

> But whoso hath this world's good, and seeth his brother have need, and shutteth up his bowels of compassion from him, how dwelleth the love of God in him?
>
> My little children, let us not love in word, neither in tongue; but in deed and in truth. (1 John 3:17)

He asks, how can one express love to God if he does not act in a loving way to people around him? Then John takes it another step by asking,

> If a man say, I love God, and hateth his brother, he is a liar: for he that loveth not his brother whom he hath seen, how can he love God whom he hath not seen? (1 John 4:20)

Loving others who are visible, tangible and physical is a measure of one's psychosexual maturity. Those who do express love to God while they hate brothers, 'love' Him on a fantasy level. Fantasy is easier than day-to-day action *vis-à-vis* others. But fantasy is not a mature, responsible, active love. We therefore conclude that spiritual growth goes no further than psychosexual development.

Our fifth principle is that the believer helps or hinders his own spiritual growth. We will discuss how he can help himself in the next chapter.

In this chapter we will focus on specific areas in which the Holy Spirit effects change, through psychological transformation. By such an analysis we take the risk of reducing man's complexities to oversimplifications and perhaps even missing the essentiality of the point. However, this analysis is necessary in order to emphasize first one and then another aspect of the psychic functioning and how change happens. It will be like looking at the changing facets of a revolving diamond in the sun's rays.

Without claim for their order of importance, we list here the components of the personality/soul in which changes are made. The importance will vary from individual to individual, depending on the personality makeup and where the Lord chooses to work with each one.

(1) Progressive identification with God: conscience revision.
(2) Memory healing: memory traces in the central nervous system made over.
(3) Ego strengthening.
(4) Unconscious material deleted and conflicts resolved.
(5) Self-image enhancement.
(6) Reintegration of forces or drives.

Progressive Identification with God

The Scriptures affirm in an assuring way, "For whom he (God) did foreknow, he also did predestinate to be conformed to the image of his Son, that he might be the firstborn among many brethren" (Rom. 8:29). But how does one go about being conformed [being molded to] to the image [likeness] of His Son? As "partakers of the divine nature" (2 Pet. 1:4), believers to some extent already are clones of Jesus. But how to finish the job? What is the process?

Let's go back to the conscience, its formation and function. The conscience is formed from the ego by a process of *identification* based on *introjection*. We find it relevant to examine this process in detail because of its importance in spiritual growth.

> In its fullest sense, the process of identifying with an object is unconscious, though it may also have prominent and significant preconscious components; in this process the subject modifies his motives and behavior patterns, and the self representations corresponding to them, in

such a way as to experience being like, the same as, and merged with one or more representations of that object; through identification, the subject both represents as his own one or more regulatory influences or characteristics of the object that have become important to him and continues his tie to the object; the subject may wish to bring about this change for various reasons; an identification may acquire relative autonomy from its origins in the subject's relations with dynamically significant objects. (Schafer, 1968)

This quotation summarizes a very important process, one which has occurred in every person during his early childhood years, and one which is experienced again following salvation: Identification by introjection.

Following birth, the biggest and most immediate task for both the mother and child is to form a unit in which there is a 'psychological fit.' Because of the thousands of interactions they will have together, this fit or bonding is essential for the child's psychosexual development. At birth the child knows nothing of the reality of this world or how his environment is constructed. This is also true of a spiritual baby. Babies exist at first only to be served.

As the child grows older, his developing concept of reality and what the outside world expects of him undergo constant change. This occurs in every person's life over a period of years. It happens so gradually that we seldom consider the vastness of the change. When we think of how extensive this world is and how tiny a receiver the baby is, we begin to appreciate the immensity of this ongoing challenge to the infant. As he recognizes more details of his environment, he responds more to it, especially to the persons who are closest to him.

The Role of Parents in Progressive Identification with God

The parents are the prime molders of their child. They are the 'reality presenters.' They may express it thus, "Well, in our family we do things *this* way. The Joneses may do it another way, but this is best for us." In the first years the parents' expectations are reinforced with physical discipline. "Foolishness is bound in the heart of a child; but the rod of correction shall drive it far from him" (Prov. 22:15).* Later, as the child acquires speech and judgment, he can be reasoned with; discipline then shifts to verbal reproofs. "The rod and reproof give wisdom: but a child left to himself bringeth his mother to shame" (Prov. 29:15).

Left to himself, the child develops no conscience, or at least a weak conscience, going through life openly transgressing against others. He may have to be bailed out of jail, bringing shame to both parents. But, "Correct thy son, and he shall give thee rest; yea, he shall give delight unto thy soul" (Prov. 29:17). Discipline by the parents pays off for both parents and child later.

Through his experiences with his parents, the child begins to observe a number of parental responses, ranging from pleasure and acceptance to anger and displeasure. How do these parental responses affect the child so as to become his eventual internal guidance? An analogy might illustrate the connection. Ever see a developing child testing objects to see how they taste? Every one is popped in his mouth for sampling. He determines that objects, with a pleasant taste, whether toys or food, are 'good.' If they are unpleasant, spicy or astringent, he determines that they are 'bad,' and spits them out. Edibles which he determines are good he swallows and they are digested to become part of the child's body. They form part of his cell structure, his body using them for building blocks.

Consider the child's experiences with his parents as capable

---
* See also Proverbs 13:24; 19:18; 23:13

of being psychologically swallowed and incorporated into his psychological structure to form the building blocks of his conscience. The technical term for this process is *introjection*. In introjection, pleasant experiences are deemed 'good' and the person gives himself approval for doing these. Unpleasant experiences are deemed bad, harmful, primarily because the parents' disapproval in the form of slaps, frowns, or angry words stirs anxiety in the child. Taken into his memory bank, anxiety 'stamps in' the experience. It forms part of behavior unacceptable to the child because of the painful anxiety he has experienced. This is the basis of the proverb, "The burned child dreads the fire!" By the process of introjection, then, the child's conscience is built.

Experience upon experience, the parents mold the child by their responses to his behavior, until the child begins to respond as they desire. We can see that the conscience is really the "inside parent(s)." The love and approval given by the parents become the persistent psychological force in molding the conscience in much the same way butter is molded from buttermilk fleck by fleck by fleck until it begins to coalesce into a solid form.

Once the conscience is formed, it becomes a part of the internal guidance center, even in the parents' absence. This point is important to understand. Someone has said, "The conscience is the price of the parents' love." The core of this ongoing process between parents and child is formed by the age of six or seven. How wide a range of behavior the person allows himself as an adult depends on his parents' latitudes, whether they concern sexual, emotional expression, eating, or other behavior.

Keep in mind that this process occurs in the context of a physical/emotional relationship. Have you ever seen children dressing up in their parents' clothes, parading up and down in oversized shoes and garments? They are identifying with the parents. Have you ever heard a young boy, being chided by his mother for some behavior, retort, "That is the way daddy does it!" These children are busy incorporating parts of their parents to become permanent parts of themselves, parts such as significant expressions, behavior, and emotional limits.

We have said the child identifies with the parents (object) both consciously and unconsciously. He does this by modifying his behavior (what he would like to do) and motives in such a way as to be like the parents. Often, this modification is difficult for the child. He gives up unbridled expression of his impulses at times in his process of socialization modeled after the parents. Once this pattern of tying himself to the parents is established ('tying' means resembling in one or more ways), it brings rewards not only to continue but to increase the tie.

Ever heard a proud dad remark, with expansive chest, "My son is just like me"? That note of pleasure is not lost on the son who, seeking his dad's favor, then increases his efforts at identifying with his dad through introjecting the dad's significant good and bad features. Finally the child, as an adult, continues to function in his identifications even without the parents' presence. His identifications have become autonomous, functioning without being prompted externally.

Conscience formation occurs in the childhood years. But in lesser degree, the conscience continues to be formed in the adult. The difference is related to lesser amounts of anxiety in relationships during adulthood. As an adult a person usually is not as dependent on others as he was in childhood, and thus their responses to him typically stir less anxiety, less 'stamping-in' potential for conscience formation.

The superego or conscience can be changed by new introjections as late as in mature life; a convincing instance of such change is in psychotherapy where the therapist becomes partly or even wholly introjected.* In fact, this is one of the essential bases of therapeutic change. In the present time, with the need for therapy so evident, many Christians are being treated by non-Christian psychiatrists and other professionals. Psalms 1:1 says, "Blessed is the man that walketh not in the counsel of the ungodly." It would seem wise to seek the counsel of Christians in order to prevent these introjections from sinners, and to avoid identifying with their principles and behavior.

This process also takes place in adult life in marriage, where spouses are often said to resemble each other over a period of time. One way they become "one flesh" (Gen. 2:24) is through introjecting parts of each other into their psychological makeup. In the couple's relating to each other, approval and acceptance or disapproval from the spouse become molding influences. Therefore one can see the logic in not being "unequally yoked" (2 Cor. 6:14) in marriage. A person identifies with his partner; this truism formed one of the underlying principles for God's command to Israel to kill all the enemy tribes in their land. Thus eliminated, the heathen could not offer objects with which His people could identify and introject.

Transfer in Progressive Identification with God

Everything said thus far has occurred in the framework of physical relationships where people can see, hear and touch each other; where they experience each other with their natural senses. Man is finite, physical; but God is infinite and spiritual.** If he cannot see, hear, or touch God, how does one incorporate God as part of his conscience? After all, as much as he may desire to do so, man cannot have a physical relationship with God.

---

* Balint, 1968
** John 4:24

Yet God becomes that internal guidance center which sponsors certain behavior or warns against other behavior. The Scriptures tell us how:

> All scripture is given by inspiration of God, and is profitable for doctrine, for reproof, for correction, for instruction in righteousness: That the man of God may be perfect [completed], thoroughly furnished unto all good works. (2 Tim. 3:16)
>
> Study to shew thyself approved unto God, a workman that needeth not to be ashamed, rightly dividing the word of truth. (2 Tim. 2:15)
>
> So then faith cometh by hearing, and hearing by the word of God. (Rom. 10:17)
>
> This book of the law shall not depart out of thy mouth; but thou shalt meditate therein day and night, that thou mayest observe to do according to all that is written therein: for then thou shalt make thy way prosperous, and then thou shalt have good success. (Josh. 1:8)
>
> My son, attend to my words; incline thine ear unto my sayings.
>
> Let them not depart from thine eyes; keep them in the midst of thine heart. For they are life unto those that find them, and health to all their flesh.
>
> Keep thy heart with all diligence; for out of it are the issues of life. (Prov. 4:20-23)

We said earlier that at a certain age, parents begin to reprove their children verbally; first, with physical reinforcements, then with words alone. God is saying that He works the same way. All Scripture is given for *reproof* along with correction. Isn't that what a physical parent does? God is also able to do these things with words, His Word. Taking these Scriptures as a unit, God is telling His people that His Word substitutes for His physical presence, and He exhorts the believer to study to be approved, to know Him better. Moreover, He says, in effect, "Pay attention to me; I am wiser, more experienced, and stronger than you!" Again, isn't this the gist of what parents tell their children in a physical relationship? God stresses that we should relate to Him continuously, day and night, experiencing Him through His Word.

The importance of continual and constant reading of the Word for spiritual growth can be better understood now. Without reading the Word in this manner, there is no way to become a disciple and to grow spiritually. How does one develop a relationship with another person? In his presence, by sharing with him. By constant interaction! Reading the Word is being in God's presence, because the Word is spirit placed on paper, making a unique book. *As God's word is read repeatedly, it is introjected to form part of the conscience;* the person who reads or hears it interacts with God. Repetition is one of the prime principles of learning, and identification through introjection is bolstered by repetition. The more one reads the Word, the more his conscience becomes infused by God's principles of behavior.

We develop trust in the context of a human relationship by testing the other person to determine his reliability and validity. Will he do what he says he will do? And will he continue doing it; does he have integrity? In the same way we test and develop trust in God by trying Him out; by doing what he says: "But be ye doers of the word, and not hearers only" (James 1:22). By doing, by shared participation, we develop a spiritual relationship to the unseen Person in the same manner that sharing experiences with a visible person develops that relationship.

Without shared experiences, one can only make educated, and sometimes not-so-educated guesses as to what the other person is like. "Trust in [rely on] on the Lord, and do good" (Ps. 37:3). Notice the order: trust, do. One cannot do good based on a relationship unless one first trusts in the other person. So the scriptural progression is: hear, trust, do good.

Because each person has different parents, each conscience originally is formed as a result of widely differing experiences with adults. Differences in parental skills, intelligence, personality makeup, and other factors result in distortions and omissions being introduced as part of each child's conscience.

Not so with the Scriptures; they provide a consistent and standardized guideline. No matter what distortions are present in the person's conscience, God is the same for everybody. He never changes;* only one's conception of Him changes. He cannot introduce distortions!

Part of being 'conformed to the image of God' is replacing distortions in the conscience with the light of the Word. The Lord works to modify the conscience by progressive identification with Him, through His Word. The two effects of this process are in: (1) reducing its strictness in those areas where the conscience is overly strict, and (2) 'building in' new areas of prohibitions where these omissions are present in the growing believer's conscience.

Conscience Revision by Reducing Strictness

Reducing the strictness of an overly punitive, criticizing conscience breaks the shackles of legalism. Ages old, yet perhaps a new word to some, legalism is a code of conduct based on dos and don'ts, a carry-over from the Old Testament dispensation of the Law. The believer's 'permissible' conduct is codified into what you can do and what you cannot do in order to remain in the good graces of the church fathers. In some very fundamentalist denominations, legalism can be crippling. It

---

* Mal. 3:6

constitutes a virtual return to pharisaical practices.

In practical terms, legalists give more attention to 'hewing to the line' than to loving others. Legalism can extend from a massive limitation of spiritual freedom to smaller, yet guilt-provoking areas. Some denominations still put out of fellowship any believer who attends movies, wears lipstick, or indulges in swimming with members of the opposite sex. Consequently, such practices stir tremendous guilt among believers in these fellowships. Their behavior is controlled by guilt and by the threat of being thrown out of the local assembly.

I had the opportunity to treat the adolescent son of a minister from a very fundamentalist denomination. The son was acting out of rebellion against the father's rules: Don't wear a hat to church; don't express your feelings to your mother; don't smoke. The father disciplined his son by having him eat an entire pack of cigarettes, at the same time threatening the boy that he must not regurgitate them, in spite of his abdominal pain. Any infraction of his father's commandments resulted in beating with a hickory stick of sizeable proportions or with a saddle girth, until the blood ran. The son could not understand how his father could do these things or how he could go to church immediately after administering such a beating and pray for members of his congregation.

In cases of legalism, where bondage needs to be broken, we recommend reading the Word and believing its message of unconditional love. This allows the believer eventual freedom. The Holy Spirit will modify behavior by His leading.

Conscience Revision by Quickening New Areas

The second modification of the conscience as a behavioral

motivator comes when new areas of behavior are quickened, or brought into being. These replace the old patterns which grieve the Holy Spirit.* Smoking may have been an acceptable addiction in a person's pre-salvation behavior. Now, as the temple of God, the physical body is to be undefiled.** The Holy Spirit quickens to the person this truth from the Scriptures, making it a part of his conscience. But to be effectively integrated or incorporated, it must then be acted upon. To do this, the person abstains *voluntarily* from this habit, for "him that knoweth to do good, and doeth it not, to him it is sin" (James 4:17). Yet it is only the Holy Spirit, not a finger-wagging mentor, who can integrate any scriptural truth as an effective part of the conscience. The conscience becomes progressively modified through these two steps to bring the person's behavior little by little into agreement with the Word.

Initially one might "do good" to please either his earthly parents or his heavenly Parent. He bases the action on his desire for approval. As he develops the relationship, however, the desire to act in a certain way, such as loving others, will progressively be based on satisfaction from within.

Paul expressed this thought to the church at Philippi: "Wherefore, my beloved, as ye have always obeyed, not as in my presence only, *but now much more in my* absence, work out your own salvation with fear and trembling" (Phil. 2:12). In other words, Paul was saying to the Philippians that they should not conduct their behavior just to please him while he is in their midst, but they should continue to do good—loving others, etc.—working out their own salvation "for it is God which worketh in you" (Phil. 2:13). God is the One who counts, not Paul and his approval. As His Holy Spirit quickens new areas and reduces strictness in our consciences as believers, we become more able to function as mature Christians. By

---

* Eph. 4:30
** 1 Cor. 6:19

introjecting God's personality into our consciences, we act as He would. We become like Him; we grow spiritually.

Memory Traces in the Central Nervous System Made Over

Conscience revision is not the only area in which we can see evidence of spiritual growth. Healing of memories makes possible balanced growth in a healthy psyche. Memory healing has become a fast-rising and far-reaching apostolic ministry, visible in the past five years.

Some critics contend that memory healing should more accurately be labeled a counseling technique; others question its authenticity on scriptural grounds. But certainly its successful performance is a ministry. As a clinician who has watched its amazing results daily, I believe memory healing speaks for itself.*

The admonition to be "renewed in the spirit of your mind" (Eph. 4:23) implies a post-salvation transformation. Only by being "transformed by the renewing of your mind" can one "prove what is that good, and acceptable, and perfect, will of God" (Rom. 12:2). Only through that transformation can one divest himself of the old programing in his mental functioning. Salvation provides the availability, memory healing provides the mechanics of that change because the 'old man' seems composed of the old sin-nature and one's memories of previous experiences. Throwing out the old memories accomplishes part of the transformation.

Satan creates bondage; thus painful memories serve the kingdom of darkness. "Where the Spirit of the Lord is, there is liberty" (2 Cor. 3:17). Memory healing, with its liberation from the past, breaks bondage to the past, to the hurts from the way a person has been treated. It provides the freedom to respond to others in the reality of present relationships.

---

* McDonald, 1980

Man's humanity is bounded by the finite dimensions of matter, space, and time. He is composed of matter, he occupies space, and he is locked into a time frame. Although he lives in the present ["Now is the day of salvation" (2 Cor. 6:2)], man can relate to events which have occurred in time and to events which he anticipates will occur in future time. The anticipation of future events is called the 'time-binding' function. Developing in the early years of childhood, this capacity allows man to imagine ahead in time. For instance, you can think ahead to when you are going to receive your paycheck.

The capacity to recall past events is mediated through memory formation, which is a magnificent capacity God has given man as one of the functions of his central nervous system. Brain and spinal column comprise this communication center. Memory formation allows man to catalog, cross-reference, and recall thousands of distinct bits of information which renders him more efficient in his life.

Paul touches on this recall ability in speaking to the Corinthian church: "By which [the gospel] also ye are saved, if ye keep in memory what I preached unto you" (1 Cor. 15:2). Without the memory of Paul's preaching they could not recall the good news of the sacrifice of Christ for them. And other portions of the Scriptures speak of the function of the memory. One of the commandments given to Israel was *"Remember* the sabbath day to keep it holy" (Exod. 20:8). God says, "Put me *in remembrance:* let us plead together" (Isa. 43:26). In speaking of the communion elements, Jesus said, "This do in *remembrance* of me" (Luke 22:19). In speaking to Timothy, Paul remarks, "I have *remembrance* of thee in my prayers" (2 Tim. 1:3). Memory plays an important part in spiritual life.

Without memories, man would be unable to orient himself in time but would hopelessly start each day without the benefits derived from the teachings of preceding days. Memories allow us to profit from experience and allow us to reason,* an important part of man's function which gives him dominion over every living creature.**

Two of the primary ways in which memories are used in relating ourselves to others is the recall of both unpleasant and pleasant experiences, along with their capacity to arouse anger and happiness in the present. The Psalmist speaks of this: "They shall abundantly utter the memory of thy great goodness, and shall sing of thy righteousness" (Ps. 145:7). Anyone experiencing God's goodness in his past has every right to sing praises to Him! On the other hand, David recalls experiences with evildoers in asking God to "cut off the memory of them from the earth" (Ps. 109:15). David is speaking of the memory of his past sins when he implores God, "Lord, be merciful unto me: heal my soul; for I have sinned against thee" (Ps. 41:4). Memories have the capacity to motivate action by arousing feelings specific to the past scene. Many of us remember and cherish the day of salvation, the day God graciously washed away the burden of our sins.

People typically remember wedding days with feelings of happiness, injuries with feelings of hurt, rejections with feelings of anger. Whatever the experience, the memory activates feelings which give action. Peter conveys this thought:

> Wherefore I will not be negligent to put you always in remembrance of these things, though ye know them, and be established in the present truth.
>
> Yea, I think it meet, as long as I am in this tabernacle, *to stir you up* by putting you in remembrance. (2 Pet. 1:12, 13)

Peter knew that, by recalling the truths of the gospel to these believers, they would be motivated to action. The same is true of modern-day preaching.

---

* Isa. 1:18
** Gen. 1:26

The capacity for motivation through memories extends back to the intrauterine period of life, the time when each person was carried in his mother's womb prior to birth. Memory stamping is mediated at first through chemical reaction, then through the hindbrain which developmentally is the oldest part of the brain. They are registered in the form of feelings without mental pictures. A mother's rejection of the child begins to build into its central nervous system a conception of rejection. The concept of rejection, well-documented, is probably felt by the developing infant as "something wrong." It is a primitive sensing of anxiety.

Psychological bonding between mother and child is *the most important human attachment.* It serves as the model for all later relationships. If this attachment is unsatisfying, all later relationships will suffer accordingly. The person may well experience some discomfort when around others. The capacity for satisfying relationships which the maternal bonding gives is well-illustrated by the relationship between Jonathan and David: "And it came to pass, when he had made an end of speaking unto Saul, that the soul of Jonathan was knit with the soul of David, and Jonathan loved him as his own soul" (1 Sam. 18:1). They fought for and protected one another until Jonathan's death. But the lack of good memories of mother-child bonding often prevents spouses from cleaving to one another and becoming one flesh.

A good example of the result of this lack of bonding and the effects of its memories is illustrated by a young man I saw last week. A late adolescent, saved in childhood, he was very disappointed that he could no longer "hear from God." He felt God had turned His face from him for some unknown reason. Needless to say, he was quite distressed. The lack of hearing, however, was not in his spiritual relationship. The culprit was this very lack of psychological bonding with his mother early on, resulting in a feeling of emptiness and vague loneliness which he felt God would fill. The memories of that emotional emptiness he had experienced with his mother as a young infant continued to intrude in his emotional life.

But memories of happy experiences as well as memories of rejection motivate behavior. For healthiest development, we need the satisfaction of certain memories, and the deletion of other memories. Normal emotional development is directly related to the ratio of the number of pleasant, fulfilling memories to the number of deprived memories. The greater the number of happy memories and the lesser the number of unhappy memories, the greater the probability for emotional happiness as an adult. The deficiency which needs rebuilding is described by Balint:

> The lack of the memories of the psychological bonding leave what some call a "fault" within the person's psychological structure. It is a fault, something wrong in the mind, a kind of deficiency which must be put right. It is not something dammed up for which a better outlet must be found, but something missing either now, or perhaps for almost the whole of the patient's life. A basic fault can perhaps be merely healed provided the deficient ingredients can be found; and even then it may amount only to healing with defect, like a simple, painless scar.
>
> In my view the origin of the fault may be traced back to a considerable discrepancy in the early formative phase of the individual between his bio-psychological needs and the material and psychological care, attention, and affection available during the relevant times. The cause of this early discrepancy may be environmental such as care that is insufficient, deficient, haphazard, over-anxious, over-protective, harsh, rigid, grossly inconsistent, incorrectly timid, over-stimulating, or merely un-understanding or indifferent.*

---

* Balint, 1968

This author tells some of the reasons why people need restructuring and memory healing.

Spiritual growth through memory healing operates in two directions: 1) removing the destructive, accumulative impact of unsatisfying memories, those of rejection, hurt, deprivation and isolation with the resulting anger found as a part of such memories; and 2) providing, through the process of 'building in,' a bank of memories which were unfortunately never experienced in childhood. In the latter instance, we build in memories shared experiences, of being cared for and loved; in essence, memories of acceptance by the 'important others' in one's life.

Memory healing eradicates the roots which prevent the shedding of the love of God abroad in our hearts.* Unfortunately, one tends to respond to others primarily on the basis of his past reactions rather than to the reality of being interacted with. It works this way: A considerable number of hurts, deprivations, and rejections creates anticipation that future experiences will be as those in the past have been. This anxious anticipation causes the person to act in a way which actually brings the unwanted response. For example, a person who experiences rejection in the past anticipates it in the future. Based on this anticipation he acts distant, thereby bringing a rejection. Then he says, "Just what I thought would happen!" Or, in Job's words, "The thing which I greatly feared is come upon me, and that which I was afraid of is come unto me" (Job 3:25).

Progressively changing the memory traces allows a greater sense of relaxation along with a greater capacity to live in the present. Thus one's social skills are increased as he relates more and more to others outside himself rather than just to thoughts in his own head. Changing the memory traces also changes the

---

* Rom. 5:5

concept the person has of himself and of God, and spiritual growth is then much more likely.

Ego Strengthening

The third component changed during spiritual growth is the ego. Although the ego was discussed briefly in chapter three, a more extended discussion is in order. The ego develops progressively during the early years of childhood through interpersonal relationships; it becomes the decision-making function of the psychological makeup.

The 'unsocialized' needs of the rapidly developing infant desire immediate, self-gratifying expression. Anyone who has watched small children play has observed these needs in action. They express the id, the fleshly desires which insist "My pleasure first." These drives give little thought to whose pain or sacrifice might be required in order to give them the satisfaction they desire. Small children grab and hit and cry in order to get what they want. Their attitude says, "So what if you had to get up six times in the middle of the night—I needed you!" All they care about is that they be served.

Unfortunately, some people never develop a reasonable way of dealing with these needs, despite their age. The number of adults who continue satisfying their needs without consideration of others is astounding. This results in an immature society.

The necessity for developing a strong ego then is obvious. But it should be pointed out that 'strong ego' does not mean 'big head.' Instead it's an ego which can make appropriate decisions and can guide one's behavior in a reasonable way, regardless of the circumstances. A weak ego is really an overvalued self-image or self-concept. The development of a strong ego which allows reasonable decisions leads to the manifestation of the fruit of the Spirit,* specifically patience and self-control.

It is sad to see believers who truly love the Lord but yet have such poor ego control and functions that they not only are impulsive in their actions, but they are inconsistent, their judgment is poor and the decisions they make repeatedly leave them at the mercy of the devil (1 Pet. 5:8) or the world. At times, these people become psychotic, leading to the incorrect conclusion that they are demon-possessed. Even without this condemnation, these people feel eventually that the Lord is not working in their lives, therefore they must be less favored in His sight than others are.

Ego Development

The ego is formed in the framework of personal situations. Parents help a child make choices from early childhood, minimizing that anxiety. Insensitive parents are often unaware of the child's need for comfort and reassurance at times of increased emotional stress. Without the reassurance, the child becomes so anxious that his developing ego is overwhelmed. In such a state he cannot function to exercise his decision-making. All he wants to do is reduce the anxiety. Some of these times of anxiety are because of separations, including the deaths of people or pets. Other anxiety-producing stresses happen when parents go to work away from home, or when playmates are lost through geographical moves, or during the first days at school. Any time the child feels he needs the parents' reassurance and it is absent, anxiety multiplies.

By reassuring the child, the parents actually help the child separate emotionally from them. The child trusts himself and his own capabilities more and more. He develops confidence in himself. Prior to this stage of emotional separation the child

---

* Galatians 5:22-23

feels that the world exists for him alone; he feels omnipotent and indulges in magical thinking which believes that whatever he wants, the world supplies. One of the changes God performs is to reduce this sense of omnipotence to one of humility and dependence on His beautiful wisdom.* The basis of the idea of confession, when it means that "you have what you say with your mouth," is based on magical thinking and grandiose omnipotence. Such thinking, denoting poor ego functioning, demeans God's position in the universe and the unfolding of His plan.

As it develops, the ego enlists the aid of helpers or defenses to assist it in its decision-making function, to keep it from getting overloaded and becoming too anxious. These ego defenses, repression being the chief one, often prevent openness in our dealings with others. In one sense, they are protective; in another sense, they are obstructive.

In spiritual growth, the ego is strengthened to promote better choices in actions and behavior. "That he would grant you, according to the riches of his glory, to be strengthened with might by His Spirit in the inner man" (Eph. 3:16). The writer of these words, Paul, knew much less about mental functioning than do present-day investigators; even so, he recognized the necessity for ego strengthening among the baby churches, particularly the Corinthian and Ephesian ones. This strengthening is a promise: "Wait on the Lord; be of good courage, and he shall strengthen thine heart: wait, I say, on the Lord" (Ps. 27:14).**

God says he will strengthen your ego: "In the day when I cried thou answeredst me, and strengthenedst me with strength in my soul" (Ps. 138:3). We can ask for this strengthening because it is His will. Peter's comments seem pertinent:

---

* Prov. 3:5, 6
** See also Ps. 31:24; Isa. 41:10

> But the God of all grace, who hath called us unto his eternal glory by Christ Jesus, after that ye have suffered a while, make you perfect, stablish, strengthen, settle you. (1 Pet. 5:10)

Notice the order: Suffer, strengthen, settle.

If we pray for patience and are given tribulations, we might say, "Lord, I don't understand! What are you doing?"

James said, "Count it all joy when ye fall into divers temptations" (James 1:2). He tells us to rejoice when we are tired. God is doing something. I believe God is strengthening your ego.

By providing opportunities to make choices, God strengthens the inner man. Making the choice of trusting Him settles us, because "Thou wilt keep him in perfect peace, whose mind is stayed on thee: because he trusteth in thee" (Isa. 26:3).

Learning occurs through doing, through activity. How many times does a dad pitch a ball to his kid to teach him to hit? A hundred times? A thousand times? With each pitch, dad gives encouraging words: "Little higher on the swing!" "Keep your head down!" "Follow through!" God does the same by presenting opportunities to learn, to strengthen the ego, particularly if the learning involves making choices. In the areas of our lives where we are attempting to learn, to become strengthened, God then presents us with opportunities to exercise.

I recall a time when, in working out the worldliness in my life (not a finished process by any means), God presented me with opportunities to exercise. For instance, I was given more change than due in a business purchase. My worldly attitude would have been, "Aha, a windfall! That chump cheated himself!" But keeping the money would be dishonest. God wanted trust in Him, not self-aggrandizement.

Then it happened again. And another time. Then I said, "But, Lord, why do you keep presenting opportunities to me?"

I knew the answer. Repetition is one of the key factors in learning. In fact, the tendency to continue repeating behavior in well-established patterns is called the "stickiness of the ego." What you have done in the past, you have a tendency to do in the future. Many times, it is necessary for God to continue the opportunities for practice until our new response becomes habitual, second nature. Now there's the meaning of "I've got that down in my spirit!"

One can say, in a general way, that the ego is comparable to the function of the will, wherein one voluntarily decides choices in a practical, reasonable way; choices which conform to the Word of God instead of to our old ways of behaving. As we make choices based on an ego strengthened through the work of the Holy Spirit, we begin to 'step out on'[trust in] our relationship with God. One becomes a doer of the Word, with the result that a memory of success is formed.

We begin building a bank of memories based on a new parent relationship, the relationship with the Lord. Reading the Word of God provides interaction in the relationship on a comprehending, intellectual basis, revising the superego. Acting on the Word builds memories of the relationship on an experimental basis, just as we did with our human parents!

This seems to me to be a clear, satisfying concept. And we can see that as the Holy Spirit modifies each of the three components discussed thus far, their interactions begin to really aid and enhance each other. So we see that there is an interaction between memory healing and the strengthening of the ego, which then works in a circular fashion.

Ego Strengthening, a Function of Spiritual Growth

Strengthening the ego means that the person will make

decisions more appropriately; will have greater self-control (which includes delaying my own pleasure in favor of serving someone else); and will display patience and other virtues. In addition, feelings will seem less frightening.* Because they are, they can be openly displayed and conflicts of a short-term or chronic nature resolved with other members of one's family, including brothers and sisters within the Body of Christ. One begins relating to others more personally, makes friends more readily, and allows others to avail themselves of you as a person more often.

This is the payoff! Remember, Jesus seldom made a convert until He made a friend of the person. Strengthening the ego will allow one to make more friends, with whom he can then share the good news.

The actual process of ego strengthening on the part of the Holy Spirit operates in a demonstrable manner. For instance, in each believer there are areas which, viewed objectively, would be considered areas where sinning is chronic. Let us take two separate but dynamically related behaviors—smoking and gluttony. These are not selected in order to condemn. We chose these from among many others because they are examples easily grasped and easily visible among believers.

There are many believers who indulge in both these habits, contrary to the Word which commands against defiling the physical body, the temple of the Holy Spirit. In both cases, the believer may be satisfied to continue this behavior. Oh, he may say, half-heartedly, "I need to stop smoking," or "I really need to stop overeating," but never make serious attempts to do either. Where there is little or no concern about these habits, we could say that this behavior is *Ego-syntonic*. Ego-syntonic simply means that the behavior that you are doing satisfies you. It comes from an 'acceptable' choice made by the ego, and

---

* McDonald, 1980

you do not experience a lot of anxiety about indulging in it.

A believer may begin the process of change with a prayer, which may be heartfelt or only half-hearted. But first there has been action by the Holy Spirit inside the person. This action results in his 'coming under conviction.' The person begins to feel that the action in question is wrong.

When this happens and he continues doing it anyway, the feeling compounds, because "to him that knoweth to do good, and doeth it not, to him it is sin" (James 4:17). The person now finds himself becoming uneasy when he smokes or overeats. What is happening is that the Holy Spirit, by stirring up anxiety over guilt, begins to make that behavior ego-dystonic.

The dictionary defines the word ego-syntonic as behavior which resonates with the ego; it is in accord with, or acceptable to, the ego. Ego-syntonic behavior is accepted as part of oneself. Ego-dystonic, on the other hand, means behavior which does not resonate with the ego. It is cacophonous, literally setting up a disturbance psychologically. It stirs anxiety which may cause it to be disowned by the person, who says, "Did I really do that?"

Practically, it means that when the believer indulges in the behavior in question, he no longer feels comfortable. He now begins to feel guilty and anxious when he participates. At this point, the Holy Spirit is well on the way to converting the behavior from being ego-syntonic to being ego-dystonic. When the process is complete, the person will say *no* to either behavior because now it is not a part of what is acceptable to his ego.

It could be said that the behavior is now ego-alien, because it seems like an unwanted foreigner. There are other choices more satisfying, such as non-smoking and reducing caloric intake. The ability to make these choices now brings satisfaction from within; the ego is strengthened, although the process may take time to accomplish. Here again the time principle of growth is operative. The change in behavior may not be accomplished without a struggle, without resistance in the ego, but the Holy Spirit will continue to work until the change is completed.

Unconscious Material Deleted and Conflicts Resolved

> The Unconscious is that part of the mental functioning in which is placed a significant portion of the mental content occurring from early childhood on. All the unresolved emotional conflicts such as desires to rid oneself of intruding younger siblings or incestuous fantasies, are lodged here as is rage toward a parent, most commonly the mother, who denied the desired nurture during those critical early years. Few people realize the intensity of the child's need for the mother in those first few years, how strong the attachment to the natural mother. (Bowlby, 1969)

Oh, were most believers' attachment to Jesus that strong!

To show the strength of that bond, let us cite the case of Ernest, a young man who has made tremendous progress through his therapy sessions. He has been delivered from homosexuality. But now he has a distressing symptom, an inability to sustain an erection. This delays his seeking marriage.

Improperly called impotence, the root of this symptom is his unconscious rage toward his mother, an hysterical woman who traveled intermittently during his early years, leaving Ernest in the care of his black nanny. His rage over being "deserted and abandoned," as he says, never gained overt expression for fear his mother would physically leave him permanently, a completion of her having abandoned him emotionally. Now thirty-eight, his repressed rage still affects him. When he attempts intimacy with his fiancee, he transfers the unconscious rage to her in anticipation that she will also reject him emotionally, as did his mother years ago, and the anger interrupts the physiology of penile erection.

It has taken Ernest some time to understand the unconscious emotional connection between the two sets of events separated in time by years. Each time he became intimate with his fiancee, he responded emotionally from his unconscious as if this woman brought into his life was the mother of years ago. Lest the reader be amazed at this connection, let me add that this *type* of unconscious interference occurs *frequently in everyone's life.* Though the Holy Spirit has worked great changes, Ernest will be unable to manage a successful heterosexual relationship with his future wife until the unconscious rage surfaces more into his consciousness, enabling it to be worked through by expression of the feelings.

This patient is typical of the destructive, interruptive effects the unconscious can have in the lives of dedicated, Spirit-filled believers. Many believers contain anger from unresolved childhood conflicts in their unconscious, being maintained there by the psychological energy of dynamic repression. Remember, repression acts as a psychological force to keep unconscious emotional material pushed out of awareness. It is similar to pushing someone beneath the water while swimming; you must stay with it, bearing down actively to keep him beneath the surface.

For many years, as with this young man, anger and unconscious feelings plague the lives of believers. He did not know these feelings were there and could not understand some of his behavior before coming into therapy. At times he would

pray for hours, seeking understanding.
But God knows:

> O Lord, thou hast searched me, and known me. (Ps. 139:1)
>
> The Lord searcheth all hearts, and understandeth all the imaginations of the thoughts. (1 Chron. 28:9)

Not only does God know what is contained in each person's unconscious, He desires to change it:

> Behold, thou desirest truth in the inward parts: and in the hidden part thou shalt make me to know wisdom. (Ps. 51:6)
>
> Shall not God search this out? for he knoweth the secrets of the heart. (Ps. 44:21)

The result of this change, when it occurs, is dramatic!

> When wisdom entereth into thine heart, and knowledge is pleasant unto thy soul;
> Discretion shall preserve thee, understanding shall keep thee. (Prov. 2:10, 11)

"Trust in the Lord with all thine heart; and lean not unto thy own understanding" (Prov. 3:5) because the Lord is infallible. The unconscious is not.

Unconscious feelings which believers carry resonate in the presence of similar overt feelings in others, causing emotional discomfort and disruption of their ongoing interactions. As an example, a believer who has a lot of unconscious anger may become uncomfortable in the presence of a person expressing irritation. His discomfort may even cause him to respond angrily.

From this, let us see how unconscious anger can cause problems in witnessing to a sinner under conviction. Witnessing to such a person often results in an angry response to the person witnessing. If he then responds angrily because the 'sinner's' open expression of anger causes resonation of his own unconscious anger, opportunity may be lost! From such an example we can see that, because of the effects of the unconscious, "He that trusteth in his own heart is a fool" (Prov. 28:26).

But the rest of the verse says, "But whoso walketh wisely, he shall be delivered" (Prov. 28:26). Every child of God should humbly and earnestly entreat, "Search me, O God, and know my heart; try me, and know my thoughts: And see if there be any wicked way in me, and lead me in the way everlasting" (Ps. 139:23, 24). Sought in this fashion, relief is promised, "If any of you lack wisdom, let him ask of God, that giveth to all men liberally, and upbraideth not; and *it shall be given him*" (James 1:5, italics added). So in order to walk wisely, we look to God. Notice this verse says that wisdom shall be given; it does not say how or when.

I am convinced that one of the ways we get wisdom is in resolution of conflicts. God helps us resolve conflicts in at least three ways:

1) by deletion of unconscious material through the Holy Spirit;
2) by human instruments in a therapeutic relationship;
3) by dreams.

In the same way the Spirit of God moved upon the face of the waters* bringing order from disorganization, so the Holy Spirit** moves within each believer to bring about order. At other times, God operates through human instruments*** to accomplish the same purpose. The third method used by the Holy Spirit in effecting change in the unconscious is in dreams. Called the "royal road to the unconscious" (Altman, 1969),

---

* Gen. 1:2
** Eph. 1:13
*** I Cor. 12:9

dreams are God's night messages, alerting the believer to unconscious conflicts and presaging His desire to work them out.

There are many biblical accounts of God speaking to His children in dreams.* Whereas in the Old Testament dreams foretold events, in present-day life dreams usually serve the purpose of marking events already passed, events whose emotional effects were repressed into the unconscious, from which they struggle to escape. The correct interpretation of dreams relieves the unconscious conflict; thus exposed to the light of the Holy Spirit, the confict can be worked through for more effective behavior.

As God spoke, "I, even I, am he that blotteth out thy transgressions for mine own sake, and will not remember thy sins" (Isa. 43:25). He works in each person's unconscious to blot out, often without the believer's knowledge, the effects of past sins and of hurts. How many times have you heard someone comment, "The Lord is doing a work in my life"? and you can observe from his relaxed, changed manner and facial expression that, indeed, something is happening. Often, it is unconscious material being resolved in God's own unobtrusive, but very effective way.

The Benefits of Deleting Material from the Unconscious

The beneficial effects derived from resolving and deleting unconscious emotional content extend from the inside out, psychologically. As the first benefit, and on the most intimate level, 'strengthening of the heart' occurs. This happens along with reduction of anxiety, allowing an increase of psychological energy with which to carry on one's daily activities. Remember, emotional content in the unconscious is kept *actively repressed* by psychological energy, and this amount of

---

* Gen. 28:12; 3:5

energy needed for repression has not been available for daily living.

An analogy would be in time of war, when soldiers at the rear capture soldiers. Because they are on guard duty there, these soldiers cannot be available for front line duty where the action is. Therefore the total force stays reduced in its strength. Once the enemy captives are removed, the guards are freed for front-line duty, strengthening their offensive force.

But when the unconscious material is resolved, it frees psychological energy. The person experiences a decrease in his general tension, a tension which came from concern that unconscious material would break into consciousness.

As a second benefit, when a person is freed psychologically, relationships with others become more open. There is more peace and contentment, along with the reduced fear of one's own feelings. And finally, the third benefit is that relationships with others and with God can be seen in the light of reality rather than from the perspective of unconscious conflicts, which always distort reality. It is interesting how many believers respond to God in terms of their unconscious conflicts rather than in terms of who He really is. Here is another application of knowing the truth, and the truth giving freedom.

Self-image Enhancement

Few adults in our society possess a healthy self-image, whether they be saints or sinners. Salvation does not create automatic change in this aspect of the believer's conception of himself, although it does provide the means for the change. Self-image develops during the childhood years and self-acceptance is at its core.

Without a sense of self-acceptance, a person continues

feeling unworthy throughout his life. He is said to have a poor self-concept or self-image. In developing a sense of self-acceptance and a good self-image, the parents are all-important. Their positive, reassuring, praising comments, made in a loving atmosphere, are perhaps the single most important ingredient in a child. This approach sponsors self-acceptance. With such guidance a child learns to acknowledge his limitations and humanness. He develops an awareness of his talents and skills, and the knowledge that he exists for a divine purpose.

But how many children are fortunate enough to have parents with enough sensitivity and maturity to sponsor self-acceptance? Children in today's divorce-ridden society are fortunate if they have one full-time parent. Indeed, it seems that only a few children consistently get the affirmation they need. Hence the necessity for a great deal of self-image change, for a solid identity following salvation.

At the root of self-acceptance is a firmly ingrained idea that the person counts, that he is wanted, loved, and above all, *valued.* What better place to start this valuing process than a knowledge of the Creator's desire for the person. The natural parents, merely the human vehicles for entrance into this world, may desire the child. But how much more does God the Father, the Creator, love and value each person?

God's Love

Not even the most caring human parents can give *constant* attention, with positive feedback to the child. By contrast, the heavenly Father is always in attendance, caring, addressing, loving and disciplining. If we ask, "Father, am I really important to you?" He wants us to know that we are. The words which He told Jeremiah to speak can be applied to any of his children: "Yea, I have loved thee with an everlasting love: therefore with lovingkindness have I drawn thee" (Jer. 31:3). He cares about us from conception: "Before I formed thee in the belly I knew thee" (Jer. 1:5). To His Church He says, "Ye are a chosen generation, a royal priesthood, an holy nation, a peculiar people" (1 Pet. 2:9). God has chosen and set apart His people. Not only that, He keeps us as the "apple of his eye!" (Deut. 32:10). Anyone who has never truly felt a dad's love should thrill to that wooing!

Think about receiving the keys of the family's car from your dad. He places those shiny keys in your hand and the gesture means love, trust, mobility, status, freedom. With those wheels you can really move out! How important you feel in the family, when you hand them back after your return! Your self-image reflects your sense of importance. And you feel valued, loved.

The heavenly Father does the same! "I will give *unto thee* the keys of the kingdom of heaven: and whatsoever thou shalt bind on earth shall be bound in heaven: and whatsoever thou shalt loose on earth shall be loosed in heaven" (Matt. 16:19). Those keys of the Kingdom place the believer in the driver's seat—not momentarily—but continuously. They give authority! They denote trust and love. They confer status.

After all, an employer will not entrust the keys of his business to any but a loyal, trusted employee. Every believer is an employee—"labourers together with God . . . God's husbandry" (1 Cor. 3:9).

And did your parents help you open your *own personal* bank account? If so, remember the thrill? Finally, you could sign your own name and it was respected, valued, in the eyes of the world. Oh, the pride in taking on the privileges and responsibilities of adulthood!

Jesus has opened a bank account in heaven for every believer, a bank account cosigned by Him. It is never questioned because His signature is written in indelible, kingly red—the royal blood of Jesus flowing from Calvary! Look at the limitless spiritual authority in that personal bank account:

> Whatsoever ye shall ask the Father in my name, he will give it you.
>
> Hitherto have ye asked nothing in my name: ask, and ye shall receive, that your joy may be full. (John 16:23, 24)

In My name! In the precious name of Jesus, the authority to draw on His unmeasured resources!

If you know Him personally, you *can* ask in His name. In His name we have all power in the spiritual world. Paul warned the believer about the battle in the heavenlies.* In combating this wickedness, we can claim His promise:

> Greater love hath no man than this, that a man lay down his life for his friends. . . . Henceforce . . . I have called you friends. . . . Ye have not chosen me, but I have chosen you, and ordained you, that ye should go and bring forth fruit, and that your fruit should remain: that whatsoever ye shall ask of the Father in my name, he may give it you. (John 15:13-16)

These Scriptures provide a cognitive (intellectual) understanding of an emotional truth—of God's desire to accept the person. A measure of one's love for another is the sacrifice he would make to insure that the other person would be with him. God went the distance. He took the supreme step of sacrificing His only begotten Son that each believer might have eternal communion with the Father.

People who as infants have had a minimum of love suffer tremendously in their self-image. It seems that they need a human touch, a "God with skin," a physical sensation to

---

* Eph. 6:12

enhance and integrate God into their self-image. In our experience, memory healing under the anointing of the Holy Spirit has provided this physical sensation. I can recall sessions with patients when, during the healing of their memories, their awareness of the Holy Spirit was so intense that it seemed to permeate every aspect of them, etching sharply into their memories the newness and satisfaction of God's love personally, just for them. It was not an intellectual concept, but a personal reality! On an experiential basis, these memories somehow substitute for the needed sensing of love denied in childhood which they needed for their self-image. From such memorable sessions the development of self-acceptance began in many believers.

As with the original development, the post-salvation, self-image change occurs as a result of identifying with the parent. The self-image has to be grounded, through identification, *in Him*. What does that mean? Paul says, "I know whom I have believed, and am persuaded that he is able to keep that which I have committed unto him against that day" (2 Tim. 1:12). Paul knew Him as Father, and he knew Him as the majestic Creator. Perhaps no place in the Scriptures affords a more panoramic description of God, of His majesty, than in Isaiah:

> Who hath measured the waters in the hollow of his hand, and meted out heaven with the span, and comprehended the dust of the earth in a measure, and weighed the mountains in scales, and the hills in a balance?
>
> Who hath directed the Spirit of the Lord, or being his counseller hath taught him?
>
> With whom took he counsel, and who instructed him, and taught him in the path of judgment, and taught him knowledge, and shewed to him the way of understanding?

> Behold, the nations are as a drop of a bucket, and are counted as the small dust of the balance: behold, he taketh up the isles as a very little thing. (Isa. 40:12-15)

We grasp the immensity of God, and then realize He is our Father, one so personal that He bids the believer to approach him with the intimate greeting "Abba, Father" [Daddy] (Rom. 8:15). This realization is breathtaking. Knowing God personally changes us.

Reintegration of Forces, Drives, and Structures

Each of the various components in which change can occur has been discussed: the conscience; the memory bank in the central nervous system; the unconscious; the ego; and self-image. An attempt has been made to show that growth in each of these various components occurs in an *orderly progression, over* a period of *time.* Further, incorporation of God as an identification on which to base conscience reformation shows *differentiation in structure. Form is* also *changed* as unconscious content is deleted. Building in memories *changes the size* of the memory bank.

Concomitant with the changes in each of these components is a reintegration of these structures and the forces and drives resulting from their psychological interaction. Imagine a bicycle wheel with all its many spokes. The tension on the various spokes determines its balance; truing the wheel involves placing equal tension on all spokes. As the wheel is trued, we could say that it has been reintegrated for more efficient performance. Likewise, the psychological reintegration allows for greater purpose and organization within each person's psychological functioning. His psyche is then in better balance for achieving spiritual growth.

The primary differences between immaturity and maturity seem to be purpose and organization within the person. Salvation provides the purpose, which is doing the Father's will.* Furthermore, it is His will for us to mature and bear fruit. Jesus said, "Ye have not chosen me, but I have chosen you, and ordained you, that ye should go and bring forth fruit, and that your fruit should remain" (John 15:16). Prior to salvation, healing can only be for change in function, not purpose. The implementation of this purpose requires reorganization in direction; a change from inward—feeding self; to outward—serving others. The reorganization further requires that each of the parts function in harmony to support this outward direction in purpose.

On the physical level, cancer is an apt analogy. Cancer in an organ differs from normal growth because of its lack of harmony. It does not contribute to the purpose of the organ or the body. While having the same structure as a non-cancerous organ, a cancerous organ serves its own purpose; it is uncoordinated with the remainder of the body, and its growth is not centrally directed. In short, there is no balance between it and the remainder of the physical body. Eventually, the cancerous part consumes the noncancerous part; the cancer is served rather than the purpose of the body.

Wholeness = God's Design

So it is with psychological/spiritual immaturity; one part, the ego, may be so out of balance with the other parts as to detract from the central purpose of preaching and teaching the gospel. The culprit may be old memories, or the contents of the unconscious, or one of the other areas. Reintegration restores the balance, sponsoring spiritual maturity. Rather than viewing the psychological makeup leading to spiritual maturity

---
* John 4:34

as parts, reintegration focuses on wholeness. This is an important distinction, because man's functioning unity is more than the sum of his psychological parts, important as they are.

> Suppose I asked you this question: "Can aluminum fly?" Think a moment. Can aluminum fly? I'm sure that sounds like a trick question. By itself, of course aluminum can't fly. Aluminum ore in rock just sits there. A volcano may throw it, but it doesn't fly. If you pour gasoline on it, does that make it fly? Pour a little rubber on it; that doesn't make it fly either. But suppose you take that aluminum, stretch it out in a nice long tube with wings, a tail, and a few other parts. Then it flies; we call it an airplane.
>
> Did you ever wonder what makes an airplane fly? Try a few thought experiments. Take the wings off and study them; they don't fly. Take the engines off, study them; they don't fly. Take the little man out of the cockpit, study him; he doesn't fly. Don't dwell on this the next time you're on an airplane, but an airplane is a collection of non-flying parts. Not a single part of it flies!
>
> What does it take to make an airplane fly? The answer is something every scientist can understand and appreciate, something every scientist can work with and use to frame hypotheses and conduct experiments. What does it take to make an airplane fly? *Creative design and organization.**

Just so, an ego doesn't work by itself. Memories don't work by themselves. The unconscious doesn't function in a vacuum, disconnected. Alone, the self-concept is an abstract entity. Then what does it take to make man 'work'? Like the airplane, it takes *creative design and organization.*

That design and organization is given by God. He said, "Let us make man in our image, after our likeness" (Gen. 1:26).

---

* Parker, 1980

Then sin disrupted, distorted, perverted that likeness of holiness.* Only through the reconstructive work of the Holy Spirit, causing psychological growth for spiritual purposes, can man begin to approximate once again that original likeness. Only through that reconstruction work can we, like Paul, remark: "But we all, with open face beholding as in a glass the glory of the Lord, are changed into the same image from glory to glory, even as by the Spirit of the Lord" (2 Cor. 3:18).

In the words of C.H. Spurgeon, that anointed nineteenth-century saint:

> Therefore, sinner, if you say, "I feel myself to be powerless, incapable, like one that is dead," let not that stand in your way, for God gives the Holy Spirit on purpose to meet just such need as yours. Everything that is needful to be done, which you cannot do, the Spirit of God will help you to do; and that which you can do, in a measure, but which you do very badly and inefficiently, the Spirit of God is given to help you to do, for he helpeth our infirmity. There is no strength wanted in thee, sinner; he will be thy strength. There is no good operation needed on thy part; the Holy Spirit has come to work all thy works in thee. He worketh in us to will and to do according to his own good pleasure; and then we, in consequence thereof, work out our own salvation with fear and trembling. If thou wilt but believe in Christ, thou needest not come to him with a new heart; here is the Spirit of God to give thee that new heart. Thou needest not strive to make thyself tender and humble in Spirit; here is the Spirit of God to make thee tender and humble. There is nothing that thou needest endeavor to produce in thyself, for this Divine Being, who brooded over chaos, and brought order out of primeval confusion, is ready to come and brood over thee—over thy dark, disordered, chaotic soul. He can spread his dove-like wings over it, till thou shalt come to light, and love, and life, and liberty, and joy. Oh, is not this a mercy that, inasmuch as we are

---

* Gen 3:6

weak and helpless, the promise of God is that he will give the Holy Spirit to them that ask him?*

So, with the working of that "grace [which] is sufficient" (2 Cor. 12:9), the mustard-seed-sized faith imparted at salvation,** begins to grow. First, there are tiny shoots; then buds; then blooms; finally, spiritual fruit appears, ripens, feeds others. We produce love, joy, peace, long-suffering [patience], gentleness, goodness, faith [faithfulness], meekness, temperance [self-control] (Gal. 5:22, 23). We can *love* "because he first loved us" (1 John 4:19). Joy derives from obedience to God's will. The *peace* of God which passeth all understanding*** comes from being accepted in an unconditional way—no strings attached, because Jesus says, "I am with you alway" (Matt. 28:20). Then we learn peace with our fellowman because we are in better internal balance. As we get to know Him, all the fruits increase!

Reduction of anger, and of the conflicts resulting from anger in the unconscious, brings *patience* and *gentleness*. Ego-strengthening affects relationships with others, and more appropriate choices provide a basis for practicing *goodness*. Self-image enhancement or consolidation brings *faith*. Faithfulness equals commitment and *meekness*. With the self-image in perspective, a person displays true meekness, which values oneself properly. And in the relationship to oneself, a byproduct of ego-strengthening is *self-control*.

We have not made any comments regarding changes in the old sin nature. But we believe that, contrary to belief in some quarters, it does not dissolve when a man becomes a "new creation" (2 Cor. 5:17). The old nature remains throughout the life of the believer and works against the working of the Spirit (Rom. 8:6). However, as the Holy Spirit sponsors growth, the satisfaction once experienced when yielding to the temporal

---

* Spurgeon, 1976
** Matt. 17:20
*** Phil. 4:7

desires of the old sin nature become progressively lessened and lose their savor. Sinning now holds no joy as it did formerly.

But "the love of God is shed abroad in our hearts" (Rom. 5:5) both as cause and effect. His love feeds growth, and because we grow spiritually, changing into the image of His Son, His love shines out from us. We drink from His rivers of living water, growing, blossoming, maturing, bearing fruit. We are His witness in the world.

11

How to Help Yourself Grow

> *... I have redeemed thee, I have called thee by thy name; thou art mine.* (Isa. 43:1)
>
> *Wherefore, my beloved ... work out your own salvation with fear and trembling.* (Phil. 2:12)

The Believer's Response

In response to God, who "first loved us" (1 John 4:19) and drew us to himself,* we come to Christ. The Holy Spirit reproves of sin,** pricking the heart until we seek "the earnest of our inheritance" (Eph. 1:14). We are new believers, spiritual babes, launched into life's greatest adventure. Now we can implement the abundant life*** available through our Lord Jesus Christ.

What is the believer's responsibility in this new relationship? In His invitation, "Come unto me, all ye that labour and are heavy laden, and I will give you rest," (Matt. 11:28), Jesus implied partnership, yoke-mates, if you will: "Take my yoke upon you, and learn of me; for I am meek and lowly in heart: and ye shall find rest unto your souls. For my yoke is easy, and my burden is light" (Matt. 11:29-30). If the believer be yoked with the Lord, both share as mates in pulling the joint load. The main understanding necessary, then, is each partner's responsibility.

As the Initiator, Jesus, through the Holy Spirit, supplies the means. He gives the energizing, transforming force of His love,

---
* John 6:44; "pre-salvation illumination," Lovett, 1976
** John 16:8
*** John 10:10

His wisdom, and His knowledge. He desires to impart these to each believer.

As the receptor, the believer has the responsibility of constantly observing Jesus, the Teacher. He is the Shepherd, the supreme Model. When a person comes to Christ, he becomes a student. Just like a new baby bonding with its parents, the new believer becomes close to Jesus, and he eagerly responds to the invitation of Christ, "Learn of me" (Matt. 11:29).

As with a natural parent, or from any teacher skilled in a special area, the necessity for closeness is obvious if we are to learn of Him. The verse, "All we like sheep have gone astray; we have turned every one to his own way" (Isa. 53:6), emphasizes the believer's main problem—wandering from that relationship of closeness to the Shepherd. And no teacher can model for the student in the student's absence. No shepherd can guide a sheep which follows its own path. Nor can a parent teach or model for a child when he is not there.

The implication of "Train up a child in the way he should go" (Prov. 22:6) is that the child will be learning by: (1) watching the parent, (2) imitating and perfecting the actions he sees by practice, and (3) receiving parental correction until the lessons are thoroughly learned. No teaching occurs in the vacuum of a sterile relationship; certainly the relationship with Jesus is not sterile!

The same three steps outlined here for the learning of skills based on parental modeling show up in the believer's spiritual growth. They are:

> 1. Howbeit when he, the Spirit of truth, is come, he will guide you into all truth. (John 16:13)
>
> 2. Verily, verily, I say unto you, He that believeth on me, the works that I do shall he do also; and greater

works than these shall he do . . . . (John 14:12)

3. For whom the Lord loveth he chasteneth [disciplines], . . . God dealeth with you as with sons; for what son is he whom the father chasteneth not?

But if ye be without chastisement, whereof all are partakers, then are ye bastards, and not sons. (Heb. 12:6-9)

Therefore, as we watch, He guides. As we imitate, He gives occasion for practice—in even greater works! And as we desire to learn, He disciplines.

In obedience to Jesus' command to learn of Him, how might the believer discharge this responsibility? What are his appropriate responses? In the previous chapter the proposition was set forth that the believer plays either a facilitative or an obstructive role in his own spiritual growth. He can help by the things he does; he can hinder by the things he fails to do.

Let's consider seven vital areas in which the Christian believer participates in helping his own spiritual growth:
1. Relationship with the Father
2. Baptism in the Holy Spirit
3. Memory healing
4. Deliverance
5. Study
6. Pursuit of holiness
7. Balanced life

Relationship with the Father—Nurturing Spiritual Growth

Maintaining continuity and deepening the relationship with the Father occurs through communication. The major aspects of this communication are reading the Word and praying.

As Spirit on paper, God's Word provides the most complete access and understanding of our Creator. In the Word we read about His attributes. The Word, which is fixed in heaven,* is the only infallible source of the believer's understanding of the nature of sin, its origin, God's attitude toward sin, God's attitude toward His people, our origins, our eternal resting place, and the dimensions of life as God desires us to live it from salvation to death or the Rapture, whichever comes first.

For the Christians, the Scriptures provide understanding of the fight we face, the nature of our enemy, and the armor in which the well-equipped soldier battles.** Without this protection, one can begin to see the hapless condition of the believer who does not feast upon the Word, the easy prey he presents for the devil who "walks about as a roaring lion" (1 Pet. 5:8).

Not only must the Word be read, but it must be read continuously! Have you ever been introduced to someone, felt a fondness for and wanted to know him or her better, to become more intimately acquainted? How do you go about carrying out this desire?

Usually we do it slowly, through many interactions, sharing information about each other in bits and pieces, trying to complete each other's understanding. Intimacy develops through this process of sharing.

Similarly, God does not share himself instantly. Through abiding in Him, and His Word abiding in the believer,*** God slowly, deftly, deeply reveals himself to those who desire to drink at his everflowing fountain. Anyone naive enough to think he will know God except through the process commanded in "study to shew thyself approved" (2 Tim. 2:15) is doomed to disappointment.

Not only is the Word to be read continuously, but also the way it is read is all-important. Let's look at some ways in which it can be read.

---

* Ps. 119:89
** Eph. 6:13-18
*** John 15:7

It can be read denominationally, in order to defend cherished intra-circle shibboleths and beliefs. As such, the Word becomes a two-edged sword—against brothers rather than against the world.

If read inquisitively, the Word satisfies intellectual curiosity, but not the longing of the soul to know more of the Father.

If read traditionally, for instance because "our family has always done so," it satisfies only the need for parental or group approval.

If read pridefully, the Word can be interpreted for judging others and for splitting hairs pharasaically, but no growth ensues.

If read superstitiously, it gives 'cookbook' answers, applicable to any problem but neglectful of the relationship with the One who is the Answer. A person who reads superstitiously resorts to the Word in times of crisis—for magical answers. We see this when the believer holds his Bible, lets it fall open, and the Lord 'gives' him a Scripture.

If read educationally, the Bible enables one to engage in conversations about it, to appear well-read; but the person may still be spiritually illiterate.

If read pedantically, it may make one able to spout off all the answers to trivia questions; but he may miss the true perspective.

Only through reading the Word to learn of God, to know His will for us and how to please Him, does the Word truly become "a lamp unto my feet, and a light unto my path" (Ps. 119:105). Then, beyond reading the Word, we must honor it by acting upon what we have read. In doing so, God's Word becomes real to us. 'Doing the Word' builds memories of a reliable and true Father and it renews our conscience. We have the experiential relationship which we need in order to grow.

Second Timothy 3:16 describes the purposes of the Scriptures. "All scripture is given by inspiration of God, and is profitable for doctrine, for reproof, for correction, for instruction in righteousness." These four categories—doctrine, reproof, correction and instruction in righteousness—clearly define the ends for which the Scriptures were written.

The first of these, *doctrine* or teaching, is a necessary aspect of renewing the mind. The Scriptures contain the only unadulterated teaching, the only true enlightenment, the final answer on any imaginable issue of life. We are not to conduct our lives according to feelings or idiosyncratic beliefs or prejudices, but simply according to doctrine based on God's Word. Doctrine provides the foundation which supports the framework of practical daily Christian living. Without clear doctrine, daily living is apt to be muddled. Such a life is often built on "wood, hay, stubble" (1 Cor. 3:12). I submit that the reason most Christians live joyless and defeated lives lies not so much in the enemy's attacks as it does in life lived without the stabilizing effect of doctrine.

Doctrineless lives are devoid of a spiritual compass, leaving the believer "tossed to and fro," prey to the "sleight of men" (Eph. 4:14). And, it might be added, to current fads, TV personalities, and the immature desire to see the gifts of the Spirit constantly displayed. When the Word is honored, it becomes a motivation of the believer toward godliness.

In order for its *reproof* to be successful, the believer needs to approach the Word with an open and humble spirit. Few people receive reproof graciously. They respond defensively, as if fearing criticism. Accepting reproof in a spirit of love brings maturity because "he that heareth reproof getteth understanding" (Prov. 15:32). Reproof is a spiritual antidote for the fleshly pride that so often feels itself above being challenged.

The sincere believer who desires growth knows when he falls short of the Word of God; his renewed conscience becomes the reproving agent! Reproof brings *correction,* which is a modifying of one's efforts in his behavior. We correct what we believe needs to be changed.

The fourth and final category, *instruction in righteousness,* follows naturally from correction. The payoff, the goal of Christian living, is to walk "in the path of righteousness" (Ps. 23:3). Only the Word of God is sufficient to impart such instruction.

Even in this verse we see His wisdom. He lists in order, (1) teaching, (2) reproof, (3) correction, and (4) instruction in righteousness. Ever the Master Psychologist, the One who knows how He designed man to learn, God has listed exactly the four sequential steps which any contemporary psychologist would advocate to teach a new skill!

I realized this when I took a tennis lesson from a young pro. At the outset of the session, my young mentor explained to me the rationale behind movements and form for a given stroke. In so doing he used *doctrine.* Then allowing me to try the stroke repeatedly, he used *reproof* by pointing out the flaws, the awkward and inefficient movements in my form and stroke. Third, the reproof led to *correction.* As I took heed to him, the flaws began to drop away. As a help, he modeled the correct form for me to copy. Isn't this what Jesus, the Master Modeler, does for each believer? He lets us practice over and over until the lesson is learned. Finally these three steps led to improved functioning and better performance, which more accurately imitated the teacher's form. This I saw as the equivalent to *instruction in righteousness.* Regardless of whether the new task is a motor skill, a recitation, or Christian behavior, this sequence of steps is most effective for learning it.

The first part of maintaining and deepening our relationship with God the Father comes in honoring the Word. We read so that we might *know His will,* and therefore we learn *what* to ask Him. The second part, prayer, is the asking.

> And this is the confidence that we have in him, that, if we ask any thing according to his will, he heareth us:
>
> And if we know that he hears us, whatsoever we ask, we know that we have the petitions that we desired of him. (1 John 5:14, 15)

In communicating with God in various ways, prayer is perhaps the most exciting privilege given the believer. Essentially, prayer is talking with the Creator in a personal, intimate, private way, with direct access to the throne of grace. God commands that His children come before this throne "boldly [intimately]" to "obtain mercy" (Heb. 4:16).

Prayer is essential in the believer's life! Why? How do you keep in touch with valued friends? By talking with them. How do you keep in touch with God? By talking to Him! By prayer.

In His omniscience, God knows everything about each person. "For there is not a word in my tongue, but, lo, O Lord, thou knowest it altogether" (Ps. 139:4). God is all-knowing, ever-present and all-powerful. Why then is prayer so important? We found that prayer serves the purposes of:

(a) Acknowledging dependence upon God's majesty
(b) Worshiping God
(c) Obtaining our need from God
(d) Sponsoring closeness by sharing innermost thoughts
(e) Practicing authority given the Church

Acknowledging Dependence by Prayer

First of all, prayer acknowledges by open expression the believer's dependence upon the Creator. Prayer thus humbles man's pride. Dependency on anyone in today's society runs counter to the main thrust of de-emphasis of authority of any kind. Supplicating God for any reason is an acknowledgement of man's puny powerlessness, a far cry from the One called upon, the One who flung the stars into space and keeps them there. Weakness always supplicates strength! Declaring one's weakness and dependency glorifies God, the "high and lofty One that inhabiteth eternity" (Isa. 57:15).

Worshiping God by Prayer
Prayer is an act of worshiping God. Kevin Dyson has described worship as the emotional, mental, physical and spiritual expression of man's whole being as he reaches up to God in adoration, veneration, and thanksgiving. The New Testament associates four words with worship: (1) submission (*proskuneo*)—to pay homage, to adore; (2) ascription (*doxa*)—to give honor, praise, glory; (3) consecration (*eusebeo*)—to show piety, to respect; and (4) communion (*latreuo*)—divine service, to minister to God. These four aspects which define a relationship to God are far different from the murmuring and complaining found in many prayers.

Obtaining Needs by Prayer
In praying to obtain our needs from God, it is foolish to think God does not know the needs of individuals. Prayer does not inform God, "for your Father knoweth what things ye have need of, before ye ask Him" (Matt. 6:8); prayer is acknowledging what He already knows. It is faith-building to learn that the heavenly Father knows your every need. He desires that we ask Him for these needs, because in the asking we progressively learn to separate need from want. We thereby eliminate unneeded requests from our prayers.

Asking also teaches the believer to phrase his request in a way that makes sense. A small child may stand before the family refrigerator, a stance which communicates to the parent his need for something inside. Why read his mind, though? He indicates his growth by learning to ask for exactly what he needs. God wants His children to exhibit the same growth spiritually.

Sponsoring Closeness by Prayer

One of the greatest benefits from prayer is a subjective one resulting from the feeling a person has following prayer. Regardless of whether the prayer results in an immediate change in external circumstances, through prayer God seems more real, the relationship more personal, the promises more precious. In a world marked by emotional separation and loneliness, one need never feel isolated. Through prayer the subjective awareness of God, always available, can lessen or stop the so-prevalent feeling of alienation. Beyond spiritual preparedness, this feeling of God's closeness alone is reward enough when we "watch and pray" (Matt. 26:41).

The strongest desire a person has is for closeness, a desire which is met through the reaffirmation of closeness in prayer. Unburdening oneself of emotions by their expression to another is healthy;* prayer can often be the channel for that emotional release. Committing these emotions to the Lord who "neither slumber[s] nor sleep[s]" (Ps. 121:4) eases one's tensions.** Thus a person can "be careful [anxious] for nothing" (Phil. 4:6). At its deepest level, prayer gives a secure sense of protection, again reminiscent of a small infant contentedly asleep in the parent's arms, safe and secure from all alarms.***

---

* Eph. 4:26
** 1 Pet. 5:7
*** Hoffman, "Leaning on the Everlasting Arms," from Deut. 33:27

Practicing Authority by Prayer

Learning to give orders with authority requires practice. The one who needs the practice may be a budding drill instructor, a new physician, or a believer learning his authority through Jesus.

> And I sought for a man among them, that should make up the hedge, and stand in the gap before me for the land, that I should not destroy it: but I found none.
>
> Therefore have I poured out mine indignation upon them; I have consumed them with the fire of my wrath: their own way have I recompensed upon their heads, saith the Lord God. (Ezek. 22:30, 31)

This Scripture indicates that men have power with God, power He has given them. The great power of the Church lies in prayer. The members of His Body have the awesome authority of working hand in hand with God in implementing the foreordained plan of God on earth.

Placing prayer in perspective, Billheimer views the responsibility and authority for the enforcement and administration of God's will as being placed upon the shoulders of the Church. God put His Church in apprenticeship, to practice their eternal sovereignty with Christ:

> To enable to learn the technique of overcoming, God devised the scheme of prayer. To give "on-the-job" training, God delegated to her the authority to enforce His will right here on earth. In order to enable her to acquire the character and "know-how" she will need as co-sovereign, He has placed upon her the responsibility and authority to enforce God's will and administer His decisions in the affairs of earth. (Billheimer, 1975)

This exciting new vista should stimulate each believer to a more active prayer life in anticipation of entering into full partnership with the Lord in the governing process of the universe throughout eternity.

Baptism in the Holy Spirit Aids Growth

Though disputed by various denominations as a result of Satan's divisive, internal warfare against the Church, the Scriptures clearly indicate a Spirit-filled life to be the normal Christian experience. Despite Satan's continued efforts to blind the Church about its source of power, the baptism in the Holy Spirit still shows its effectiveness in "fight[ing] the good fight of faith" (1 Tim. 6:12). The empowerments of the Spirit make us more able to prevail in our Christian warfare.

Furthermore, we are commanded to be Spirit-filled:

> And be not drunk with wine, wherein is excess; but be filled with the Spirit;
>
> Speaking to yourselves in psalms and hymns and spiritual songs, singing and making melody in your heart to the Lord;
>
> Giving thanks always for all things unto God and the Father in the name of our Lord Jesus Christ. (Eph. 5:18-20)

Properly understood, Paul tells the Ephesians not to depend on external support which will distort their lives, but on the internal Source which provides the basis for a victorious, joyous, overcoming life.

Once sealed with the Spirit, why does a Christian need the baptism in the Holy Spirit? We have just mentioned the first reason, which is a command: "[You!] Be filled . . ." (Eph. 5:18). Then, as the second reason, we see Jesus as our Model. He received the baptism to symbolize the energizing power of the Holy Spirit in His earthly existence. The occasion is recorded in Matthew: "and he [John] saw the Spirit of God descending like a dove, and lighting upon him [Jesus]" (Matt. 3:16). This leads us to conclude, as does another writer on the subject, "If our High Priest needed it, how much more do we, as His disciples, need it?" (Riggs, 1949).

So the first result of the baptism in the Holy Spirit is spiritual power, foretold by Jesus in His farewell address to the disciples: "Ye shall receive power, after that the Holy Ghost is come upon you: and *ye shall be witnesses unto me* both in Jerusalem, and in all Judaea, and in Samaria, and unto the uttermost part of the earth" (Acts 1:8). This power, then, is witnessing [martyr] power. It is marked by the increased desire to tell boldly the good news. Perhaps the effects could be compared to the conversion from a 110-volt outlet to a 220-volt outlet. We become plugged into the availability of more power.

The witnessing begins with speaking, the initial act which occurred on the Day of Pentecost: "And they were all filled with the Holy Ghost, and *began to speak* with other tongues, as the Spirit gave them utterance" (Acts 2:4). This power extends from speaking with new tongues to casting out demons, and to praying for healing the sick (Mark 16:17). These powers were presented to the Church by Jesus. He said "As my Father hath sent me, even so send I you" (John 20:21). He says to us, *with the same power send I you!*

Secondly, the baptism provides energizing and continual refilling of the Spirit, emphasized by "building up yourselves on your most holy faith, praying in the Holy Ghost" (Jude 20). "Praying always with all prayer and supplication *in the Spirit*" (Eph. 6:18) causes "the whole armour of God" (Eph. 6:11) to be more effective in spiritual warfare. Praying *in the Spirit*, sometimes called "tongues," is a private prayer language, a

'WATS line' to the Lord! Praying in one's prayer language has the same effect on the spirit as does a charge on a car battery; it completely revitalizes it! This empowerment is held in such high regard that I recommend to all my patients that they should pray in the Spirit fifteen minutes every day.

Praying in the Spirit, our third reason for desiring the baptism, opens the avenue for intercessory prayer. Often, when I minister publicly, requests are made to me for prayer. Because of my human limitations, I may not know exactly how to pray for each request or individual. In these instances, I pray in the Spirit, because "likewise the Spirit also helpeth our infirmities: for we know not what we should pray for as we ought: but the Spirit itself maketh intercession for us with groanings which cannot be uttered" (Rom. 8:26). With the Spirit, there is no thought of error. Praise God for access to infallibility! When the Lord is seeking someone to "stand in the gap" (Ezek. 22:30), praying in the Spirit may be the only practical way to do so effectively.

And fourth, the baptism allows the nine gifts [charismata] of the Spirit to operate through a person, for ministry to others,* whether for healing, faith, prophecy, word of knowledge or word of wisdom. These gifts are not for self-edification, nor are they private or permanent possessions. They are instead momentary empowerments. Manifestations of the Spirit reach momentarily beyond the range of our natural abilities, into God's mind as it were, to benefit others.

The manifestations of the Spirit therefore are given so that we may minister one to another. Jesus provided the model of ministry when He washed the disciples' feet,** taking the servant's role. Therefore, the use of these manifestations of the Spirit in ministering to others does not necessarily make us more spiritual than they. One's spirituality is not measured by

---

* 1 Cor. 12
** John 13:14

the gifts; instead Jesus said, "By their fruits ye shall know them" (Matt. 7:20).

Memory Healing Aids Growth

We have shown that the memories from childhood of negative, destructive experiences, imprinted in the mind, cause people to act destructively. Our concern in therapy is the behavior which is "enmity against God" (Rom. 8:7). This behavior detracts from Christian witness.

A married couple whom I saw, both Spirit-filled, illustrate this point. Though committed to the Lord and desiring to be led by the Spirit, they nevertheless fought continually. They feuded and cussed each other, to their mutual disgust, sadness and remorse.

Each had brought to their marriage a lifetime of memories of disappointing parents, previous marriages, and lives in general. In their fighting they were not relating to each other; instead each related to his own individual bag of memories, transferred onto the marital partner. To that point, Satan was the big winner in their marriage. Memory healing for both of them over a period of time changed two lives of misery.

Hardly anyone escapes childhood without serious psychological hurts; many sincere Christians are collections of psychological bruises, bleeding psychologically from past unhealed wounds, continually sad despite being filled with the joyful potential of the Spirit. Lest anyone pridefully think he is immune or has escaped, reflection while seeking God's grace will reveal those areas causing bondage from which the Lion of Judah can bring freedom. Rejections extending to an unwanted pregnancy, loss of parents through death or divorce, separations of various kinds, sexual abuse—the entire range of rejections to which the uncertainties of human existence expose a person—remain locked in believers' minds as motivators.

Yes, you say, but isn't forgiveness enough? Doesn't it suffice to cleanse? Perhaps, but have you ever stood at a busy intersection wearing a newly cleaned suit, only to be spattered with mud from a passing car? Following the disappointment and irritation, *and forgiveness,* was the suit renewed? Were the spots removed? No, the spots were still there until the suit was dry-cleaned again. Such are memories; the spots need to be removed from the mind. In a sense, God runs a dry cleaner for the mind! He removes the spots!

Following his rebuke by Nathan over his misdoings, in his psychological pain, David cried out, "Have mercy upon me, O God, according to thy lovingkindness: according unto the multitude of thy tender mercies blot out my transgressions. Wash me thoroughly from mine iniquity, and cleanse me from my sin" (Ps. 51:1, 2). David asked God to blot out the sin from his memory, to *heal the memories* of his past, so he could have peace and freedom.

The keys to healing then, are acknowledgement followed by seeking. "When thou saidst, Seek ye my face; my heart said unto thee, Thy face, Lord, will I seek" (Ps. 27:8). "O God, thou art my God; early will I seek thee" (Ps. 63:1). As a believer, do you go before the Lord, seeking His face for understanding and healing of your memories? If you will do so, God will answer because, "Ask, and it shall be given you; seek, and ye shall find; knock, and it shall be opened unto you" (Matt. 7:7). Therefore, if you continue having problems in a certain area, ask the Lord to show you any memories which need healing and ask for His restoration to health. Many times, memory healing sponsors amazing growth.

Deliverance as an Aid to Growth

Deliverance is the companion piece, the natural accompaniment, of memory healing. Many Christians need deliverance from an evil spirit, a demon, in a certain area of their lives. The presence of evil spirits in a person's life creates a bondage; there is a blockage which cannot be overcome through dint of an agonizing effort, meditation, or prayer. Why? Because evil spirits intrude into lives. Evil spirits are disembodied angels, cast out of heaven by God when they rebelled along with Satan, who attempted to exalt himself above God.* Like all darkness, they gain entrance in the absence of Light, either before the person comes to salvation or because of continuing wrong behavior following salvation.

In the first case, evil spirits may enter a person while he is yet unborn, similar to the Holy Spirit entering John the Baptist while yet *in utero* (before birth).** Spirits of rejection enter the unborn child when the mother withdraws her emotional covering from the child. Or later, spirits of anger, jealousy, and a host of other spirits can enter the child because of other people's actions toward him; in effect, as the result of sin.

The opposite of these, the Spirit of love, comes only through the acceptance of the Lord as Savior.*** But once evil spirits have entered, the person is 'locked in' with regard to certain behavioral responses. For example, once a spirit of rejection enters, that person cannot help but feel rejected often, even in the most benign circumstances. His responses are influenced by the evil spirit.

Salvation does not provide automatic insurance against evil spirits. Paul cautioned, "Work out your own salvation with fear and trembling" (Phil. 2:12). Part of the "working out," the daily implementation in practical living, is living according to the Word, in displaying love by one's actions to others.****

---

* Isa. 14:13
** Luke 1:15
*** John 3:16
**** John 13:14

But fighting the good fight of faith "against spiritual wickedness" (Eph. 6:12) is also part of the battle. Clearly, the transformation in a Christian's life is purposefully resisting the old tugs of the flesh. One needs to fill his being, his psychological house, with the Word of God. The possible plight of the believer who fails in this important task is illustrated in the following passage:

> Then he [the unclean spirit] saith, I will return into my house from whence I came out; and when he is come, he findeth it empty, swept, and garnished.
>
> Then goeth he, and taketh with himself seven other spirits more wicked than himself, and they enter in and dwell there: and the last state of that man is worse than the first. (Matt. 12:44, 45)

Once they indwell a believer, evil spirits do not leave willingly. In vesting His disciples with overcoming, world-changing power, Jesus said the attesting signs of His believers were in part, "In my name shall they cast out devils [demons]" (Mark 16:17). The numerous scriptural passages citing Jesus delivering people from evil spirits speak of "casting out" or "driving out" (in the Greek, *ekballo*), but never "away from."* Therefore the evil spirits were *within* people, and only the authority over Satan given by Jesus suffices to go within and counter and expel those evil spirits.

There is no passive immunity against evil spirits. The places of attachments for evil spirits seem to be the blocks of unhealed memories where feelings are 'tied up' in the mind. But following resolution through memory healing, evil spirits have no natural or rightful attaching place. They must leave when commanded. Some spirits, of course, may be commanded to depart without extensive memory healing. Our desire is to focus on relieving from bondage rather than any specific

---

* Matt. 7:22-23; 8:28-34; 10:1; 10:8; 12:22-30. Mark 1:34, 39; 3:15; 6:13; 16:9, 17. Luke 11:14-26; 13:31-33

technique. God cannot and will not, I believe, be placed in a box, subject to human conditions.

The believer should seek deliverance when he is led to do so. It is sad to see believers still in bondage to evil spirits when, for the seeking, they can be set free! Seeking deliverance is a voluntary step. While one can pray for deliverance by oneself, ordinarily the ruling spirits are so entrenched that the agreement of a brother* may be necessary for successful deliverance. One who has a ministry of deliverance may also be helpful in discerning the particular troublesome spirit(s). One must first be aware of such a problem in order to then be ready for this step which can help him grow.

Bible Study Courses for Growth

In addition to daily private reading of the Word, there is the necessity for continued learning in the form of formalized Bible study. As a help, commentaries such as Henry's or Ryle's are available. They expand on biblical passages. Many churches offer ongoing Bible courses as an integral part of their Christian education program. Some Christians are fortunate enough to be in a church where they can obtain instruction in every area of the Bible, extending from Hebrew and Greek to hermeneutics. In the absence of such classes, the same program might be studied by correspondence courses, seminars, or prepared instruction such as cassette tapes. God quickens the Scriptures to a believer in individual reading and meditation, but teachers who administer their gift to the church body** are invaluable for concentrated study of the Word. And in turn, study of the Word feeds the Christian so that he grows.

Pursuit of Holiness as an Aid to Growth

The pursuit of holiness is a necessary activity if we are to

---
* Matt. 18:19
** Eph. 4:11

grow spiritually. Holiness is commanded by God: "Sanctify yourselves therefore, and be ye holy: for I am the Lord your God" (Lev. 20:7). Holiness means separating oneself from evil and evil associations.

Pursuing holiness cannot be done without mortifying the flesh: "Mortify therefore your members which are upon the earth; fornication, uncleanness, inordinate affection, evil concupiscence, and covetousness, which is idolatry" (Col. 3:5). This mandate concerns individual responsibility. Each one of these "members" must be decided against by the individual, every time it presents itself. So in each of these areas mentioned in Colossians 3:5, as well as in any other where one is apt to sin, deciding not to heed the urge must be practiced. It's easier to yield when tempted if we put off standing fast until 'the next time.' Such an action flies counter to the way the mind works. Once we yield, it is easier to yield the next time, rather than to stand. One might even yield on successive occasions with less and less guilt. In fact, Paul tells Timothy of some "having their conscience seared with a hot iron" (1 Tim. 4:2). And once the conscience is seared, guilt becomes decreased through the defense mechanisms of repression and denial. Of course we know that this is not the way to reduce guilt. We must not just repress it. Instead we put to death (mortify) the deeds of the old sin nature. We change our behavior!

Have you, as have other believers, said to yourself, "I can't do that. I can't change my behavior. The task is too difficult!"? But think—the issue is responsibility for your own actions. Can I see myself as responsible for what I do rather than using the excuse, "The devil made me do it"?

"Likewise reckon ye also yourselves to be dead indeed unto sin, but alive unto God through Jesus Christ our Lord. Let not sin therefore reign in your mortal body, that ye should obey it in the lusts thereof" (Rom. 6:11, 12). These Scriptures tell believers that Jesus has accomplished the victory over sins and Satan. Not allowing sin to reign is the action of will which each believer must take. When he can reckon himself dead to sin and alive to Christ the decision *not* to yield becomes easier and easier.

Therefore, pursuing holiness requires constant and vigilant practice over a period of time. There is that time dimension of growth again! Sin habits, like multiplication tables, are so over-practiced that time is required to unlearn them and to substitute instead the practiced habits of holiness.

Spiritual Growth in a Balanced Life

For proper physical/psychosexual growth we need balance in our lives. Because all growth is governed by laws common to all aspects of our lives, we need the same balance for spiritual growth. Let's look at the factors involved in both.

For physical/psychosexual growth, a close bond with our parents nurtures us. Then, we receive what we need for the care of our bodies and souls, and eventually we are able to do the same for others. We sleep and wake, secure in the love of those who care for us.

We laugh and cry and build good memories, and grow still more. Parents keep us from harm and teach us to spot evil and to combat it. We study, growing in knowledge. We practice and experience, growing in wisdom. We become morally strong, learning to refuse things that would harm us. And so we grow tall and straight and strong and able to nurture others.

Spiritually, we have the same aids to growth available to us, and we can have them in balance. Our heavenly Father wants us to develop a close bond with Him. He also gives us gifts. They are both for our provision and so that we may minister to others. As our parents "know how to give good gifts . . . how much more shall your Father . . . give good things to them that ask him"(Matt. 7:11). Therefore, as we come to know our Father better, we find we can ask for and experience His provision for us; and we can work and rest, secure in His love.

Yet sometimes we find that, in spite of accepting all of His gifts and endeavoring to grow in grace, we still make little progress in spiritual growth. Some people are quick to point to some underlying sin, others to a lack of faith. This is not necessarily the case or the whole truth.

Because none of us has the ideal situation all of the time in our formative years, we may need healing and further instruction in order to mature more fully. This is true both of physical/psychosexual and of spiritual growth. In fact, since spiritual growth equals psychological change, our spiritual development may be stymied by a psychological difficulty which needs to be worked out.

For better spiritual growth we can rebuild our memories. We can be delivered from evil. We can also learn to fight it by using the authority we have over Satan and by refusing evil consistently, thereby strengthening our wills. And we can study, taking our sustenance from Him who is the Bread of Life. Our goal is to grow straight and strong and to be able to help others.

Although we can help ourselves grow, we are not islands unto ourselves. We need the help of others. Many of us do not hesitate to seek help for deliverance or for the study of the Word.

So each believer needs to determine within himself, by reviewing his life and progress, whether he needs to seek professional help. Many people deny themselves needed treatment by denying the seriousness of a problem. They may misunderstand its source and blame it on the devil. Some believe that they have no choice but to agonize over a problem and coexist with it. They call this 'suffering for the Lord's sake.' Unfortunately, they do not know the peace and freedom available with good psychological treatment.

Just a word more about this. In some quarters, seeking psychiatric treatment is not fashionable. Indeed, some pastors inveigh against it, even though God has placed those who do such ministry in the Body of Christ, the Church. Yet often the ones who preach against therapy are the ones who would not hesitate to seek deliverance from evil spirits.

If all of these objections to getting help from others in the professional field are removed, the underlying concerns appear to be financial or perhaps the fear of dependency which a therapeutic relationship raises. In our next chapter, then, we will discuss the difficulties and the benefits of therapy while we look in more detail at some of the ways others can help us grow.

12

Others Can Help You Grow

But grace was given to each of us according to the measure of Christ's gift . . . . And his gifts were . . . to equip the saints for the work of ministry, for building up the body of Christ, until we all attain to the unity of the faith and of the knowledge of the Son of God, to mature manhood, to the measure of the stature of the fulness of Christ; . . . speaking the truth in love, we are to grow up in every way into him who is the head, into Christ, from whom the whole body, joined and knit together by every joint with which it is supplied, when each part is working properly, makes bodily growth and upbuilds itself in love. (Eph. 4:7, 11-13, 15, 16—RSV).

Human Support Systems

Throughout this book we have placed our emphasis on the energizing, growth-actuating properties of the Holy Spirit. Praise God for Him! Grieved at times, quenched all too often, the Holy Spirit still works in believers' lives, forming, molding, and transforming.

In times past, the Holy Spirit worked in diverse ways to accomplish His desired goal. The tool or method He used was always natural and appropriate to the circumstances. In the hands of a shepherd boy, an insignificant sling won the day. In the hands of the strong man, Samson, the jawbone of an ass won the victory. In the hands of Ehud, an oxgoad slew six hundred men.* At other times, even the elements were the tool of deliverance or victory.

God has always worked through people to 'bring in the kingdom.' In the Old Testament, prophets spoke to His people as a group, proclaiming the Lord's word. They also spoke to people singly for a specific purpose, as when Nathan confronted David regarding his flagrant sin, or when Elisha spoke to Naaman for healing of his leprosy.** In each case, men did the speaking, the Holy Spirit did the work!

In modern times, extended hands continue to implement God's plan. Indeed, ministering one to the other fulfills God's plan in the best New Testament sense. Clericalism, the manmade distinction between clergy and laity, continues; yet beyond the administrative post of pastor, God intended every true believer to minister one to another. He gives each of us a special ministry whose development strengthens and benefits the entire Body.

This work would be incomplete without a concluding chapter on human support systems built into the Body. We use the term, human support system—perhaps new to some readers—simply to mean those resources, formal or informal, through which God carries out His heavenly, preordained plans. As I see it, God entrusts His tasks to His children for two reasons: To teach authority for the time when we will "reign with Him," (2 Tim. 2:12); and to unify the Body as "an holy temple in the Lord" (Eph. 2:21). The New Testament records human support systems most clearly in the Acts (of the Holy Spirit through the Apostles): "And they, continuing daily with one accord in the temple, and breaking bread *from house to*

---

* 1 Sam. 17:49, 50; Judg. 15:15; Judg. 3:31
** 2 Sam. 12:1-7; 2 Kings 1-10

house, did eat their meat with gladness and *singleness* of heart" (Acts 2:46). "And daily in the temple, and in every house, *they ceased not to teach and preach Jesus Christ"* (Acts 5:42). These passages illustrate the unity of the family of Christians through continuous accord and ministry, which led to singleness of heart, to common purpose and unity of the believers.

The book of Acts is incomplete in the sense that each day the acts of the Holy Spirit continue. These could be thought of as Acts, chapter 29. Indeed, the Holy Spirit must still work through us, giving support to one another, for God's work to flourish.

A part of the human support system for Christians has been the rise and increasing spread of Christian counselors and therapists. In the New Testament, Christians broke bread and ministered to one another. Today we follow that tradition. As knowledge of psychological functioning has become better understood, counseling and psychotherapy, performed according to biblical principles, ministers to special needs in the Body. It is the contemporary extension, with sophisticated methods, of New Testament breaking of bread and ministry.

To their detriment, many Christians procrastinate in seeking therapy. Having 'waited on the Lord' for years, they only continue in psychological agony. The problem, however, is not the Lord's. The delay is motivated by reluctance to allow the Lord to minister according to His chosen method in any given case. They limit God by setting false standards for themselves.

A lady called from a neighboring state, seeking an appointment. Her conversation, marked by depressed and despairing tones, told of this agony, ending with "You are my last hope." What an awesome responsibility to place on a member of the human support systems! Without the energizing of the Holy Spirit, this ministry of therapy is an unenviable challenge. But in her desperation she had finally turned to this type of human support system.

She had not realized that we use Jesus as our model. Healing in many ways, He ordered treatment by commanding a leper to wash in a pool; He put his fingers in a man's ears; He rubbed spittle mixed with mud over another's eyes; and sometimes He spoke words only.* Whatever the time dimension, whatever the method, no matter through whose hands, *healing is of God, has its source in God, and occurs only through God.* For instance, it does not matter who prays for healing. Whether it is Billy Graham, Oral Roberts, or a small child, the Holy Spirit does the healing, either supernaturally or by releasing various internal blockages which prevent the body's properties from nurturing the growth it was designed for originally.**

Earlier, the statement was made that the believer acts as a facilitative or obstructive agent in his spiritual growth. God expects us to work with Him; often, however, the believer obstructs God's hand in his behalf through either his lack of dependence, or through his lack of commitment. In each case he dilutes his relationship with God, perhaps to a casual one.

Why do some Christians need therapy to resolve their problems, therapy exclusive of the Holy Spirit's working solo in their lives? The reasons, perhaps an incomplete listing, are summarized without regard to any particular order of importance:

Need for a personal relationship
Lack of introspection
Lack of psychological sophistication
Lack of discipline
Denial
Availability and/or cost
Crisis intervention
God's omnipotence

---

* John 5:2; Mark 7:30; John 9:6; Matt. 9:22
** Ps. 139:14

Need for a Personal Relationship

Some Christians seem to need a human, personal relationship as a framework in which growth may occur. Remember, the initial interpersonal framework was mother-child. Week after week in the office I hear stories of destructive parental treatment toward children who, now as adults, find life barely manageable despite being saved and Spirit-filled. In less severe cases, noticeable limitations in various areas of their relationships are evident.

For example, Jim, a late-adolescent male, ran afoul of the law by breaking and entering. The son of a pastor, in the course of his treatment he has recalled many instances of being beaten with a horse girth or a stout stick until he bled, then being threatened by his dad not to reveal his bruises when he went to physical education classes. Jim had been damaged by this destructive personal relationship.

In other cases, patients have little or no identity, little idea of who they are as people, as individuals; they have little idea of self. In particular, schizophrenics suffer from this lack of identity; in addition, they have poor control over their feelings, and difficulty in decision making. Some reliable estimates place five- to ten-percent of the population in the schizophrenic category. Because of their confused thinking, schizophrenics possess poor judgment.

Many of the out-of-order messages spoken in public assembly are delivered by believers with poor reality testing. These people are unable to test reality with any degree of surety; to distinguish between flesh and spirit.

Mrs. Kelly, a lady who presented a glowing story of her previous closeness with God, illustrates this point. In her Bible reading, God had instructed Mrs. Kelly not to eat with her family after preparing a meal for them. Instead, she was to "come aside" and "feed on Him." Later, she felt no desire for sexual relationships with her husband, but felt cleaner by "fellowshipping with God." But she did not hear her messages from God; her confused thinking about closeness and cleanliness resulted from her schizophrenic disorder. To an outsider, her amount of time spent in the Bible may have seemed like genuine spirituality.

True believers feed from the Word, desiring first "milk" and then "meat" (1 Cor. 3:2). But they do not confuse spiritual eating, feeding one's spirit, with literal eating for physical nourishment. Often, schizophrenics search for a mystical relationship with the Lord in a misplaced attempt to heal that basic fault from a faulty mother relationship. They become angry with God because they cannot 'feel His presence.'

These people, as well as others with lesser degrees of ego impairment from destructive childhoods, grow most quickly in a therapeutic relationship. Testing reality with another person skilled in this area helps sort out their confusion and perplexity which reaches the point of not being able to hear God accurately. From hours of observation and therapy, my conclusion is that the more emotionally deprived the person's childhood, the more a personal relationship is needed to foster a sense of trust and the feel of human love. One goes from a psychological being to a spiritual being, not vice versa. Until one has basic experience in sensing humanness, he is poorly equipped to love an unseen, but loving heavenly Father. The ability to feel love seems to occur basically within the boundaries of interacting with another human being.

Lita, whose therapy covered three hundred hours, is a good example. Though Spirit-filled, she had no sense of who she was at the beginning of treatment, no sense of trusting or loving others, despite having prayed over her condition many times.

She sensed something was wrong with her; in fact, she sensed a 'basic fault,' but knew no name by which to call it.

In her therapy, she gradually learned to love; slowly, ever slowly, agonizingly so at times, she learned to trust and love as her ego function improved. With every gain, she could recognize more clearly what her deficiencies had been before, the lack of love she had cried about. As she developed her sense of love, first for herself as an individual, then her family members, this new capacity was then opened (transferred) to her heavenly Father. But *not before.* Then, the "dry bones" (Ezek. 37:4) began to come to life, having developed 'spiritual flesh' through the human relationship.

Lack of Introspection

In dealing with God, as with a human parent, one is expected gradually to begin asking for his needs, rather than having them met as a matter of course. We not only learn to acknowledge dependence on the Father, but also learn to communicate with Him. But we don't know what to tell Him until we can identify our problems.

Discovering and asking God to resolve areas of emotional conflict in one's life requires *introspection,* literally a looking into oneself psychologically. The ability for introspection varies greatly from person to person. Some see cause-and-effect relationships in their dealings with others quickly and easily; others, poorly or not at all. Some grasp quickly what they are doing psychologically and why, what significance it has for the earlier experiences they may have had with others, such as parents. James said, "Ye have not, because ye ask not" (James 4:2). This infers that some may not know what they need because of their inability to look into themselves.

Lack of Psychological Sophistication
Introspection, therefore, relates to psychological sophistication, to a knowledge of what makes a person 'tick.' Many people can work with God as He reveals things about themselves, using each revelation or insight to change their behavior, their non-willful sinning. Believers who have difficulty introspecting or who have little skills in examining and understanding themselves may not benefit from the Holy Spirit's desire to reveal facets of themselves for change. If so, there may be a necessity for a therapeutic relationship in which psychological truth can be pointed out by a visible teacher.

Ministering to others involves a sensitivity to their needs, a sensing of where they are psychologically when dealing with them. Jesus ministered in a different manner to Nicodemus than to the woman at the well.* He ministered from His sensitivity to their hurts and needs. In effect, He ministered from His psychological sophistication and discernment. Since we are commanded to minister, I believe God would have us increase our psychological sensitivity in order that He might use us more effectively and extensively.

Introspection requires the capacity to bear psychological pain, to feel the anxiety inside oneself and to bear with it. Many people tolerate the internal pain so poorly that it interferes with probing into their own inner workings. Yet God is most interested in the working out of each person's salvation. He is concerned with our desire to accomplish this process of change through His transforming ability.

Lack of Discipline
Learning psychological sensitivity and introspection requires discipline, one of the backbones of Christian life. Even

---
* John 3:1-21; John 4:1-30

those believers who, like sheep, have gone their own ways,* are not denied growth and change in their lives. God can teach them discipline through a therapeutic relationship.

Developing discipline is one of the marks of Christian growth. Discipline is consistency, the ability to persevere more than on a piecemeal basis. Discipline is necessary to "fight the good fight" (1 Tim. 6:12). Paul compares the Christian fight to one in which many start but soon become spectators who never obtain the prize.** The disciplined believer continues, continues, continues on a daily basis. He displays an essential personality ingredient against the adversary, one of whose chief strategies is discouragement. God might well direct undisciplined believers into a human support system where they can be taught and can practice this valuable trait.

Denial

One of the primary ego defenses frequently used by believers is denial. You know the scene: The person says, even when walking with a limp or in obvious pain, "Oh, nothing is wrong with me." Such a response is an example of denial, which is pretending that nothing is wrong. To some, constant denial is a way of life, hindering their relationships with others and with God.

When someone who is obviously angry says, "No, that doesn't bother me at all," we can see that denial is a form of dishonesty, an ego defense which needs to be transformed by the development of openness and trust. Openness will allow the person to say, "Yes, I'm angry." And a trusting relationship will let him or her talk it out or resolve the problem with whoever else is involved.

I know a divorced lady, dedicated to the Lord, who is such a constant user of denial that it hinders her life. She wants a

---

* Isa. 53:6
** 1 Cor. 9:24-27; Phil. 3:14

husband, a companion, desperately. She fusses at God because He doesn't answer her prayers in this regard. But actually, she is not ready for a husband; she refuses dates, vowing God can "bring a man to my door!" Doubtless, He can. But why not socialize, fellowshipping with others? Why put all the responsibility on the Lord? She has tried many churches and prayer groups, but finds fault with all of them eventually. Despite all this, she persists in denying that she needs help in her psychological problem areas, or that she needs therapy.

Poor old God; it is all His fault! She has been so faithful, but He just won't do anything for her! In our last brief conversation, she told me that she had almost quit praying, a dangerous way to deal with anger toward the Lord.

The Word says, "Is any sick among you? let him call for the elders of the church . . ." (James 5:14). For healing, it is first necessary for the person to acknowledge that he or she is sick. If we are angry, we need to recognize and confess our anger, and the reasons for it, to Him. When believers persist in denying problems in their lives, God may move them into human support systems in order for them to have it pointed out to them more directly, clearly and persistently.

Availability and Cost

The number of trained, Spirit-filled personnel, even at this time, is still limited in the counseling area. There are probably no more than twenty-five Spirit-filled psychiatrists over the entire country who allow the Lord to direct their therapeutic activities. There are a greater number of Spirit-filled psychologists. The sum of all Spirit-filled, trained counselors still leaves many believers without access to such support systems. And for those fortunate enough to have easy access to trained counselors, cost functions as a potential deterrent to seeking help. But God is increasing the number of such therapists. And I believe, for those whom He directs into this kind of help for their growth, He will provide the finances. He owns the cattle on a thousand hills (Ps. 50:10).

At least one support system in the form of a retreat for ministers and their wives has sprung up in Colorado under the guidance of its psychiatrist-founder. Of help to many sore-pressed pastors already, "Still many clergyman don't take advantage of the program because of the attitude that ministers are above needing such help. But one pastor, after completing the two-week therapy session, said: 'There are those who say that we should realize our God works through people—otherwise why would anyone go to a pastor for help?' "*

Crisis Intervention

Some circumstances in believers' lives reach crisis proportions. For one believer, it may be the death of a loved one; for another, a divorce; for another the catastrophic loss of his home. These events may tip the psychological balance in the person, a balance which already may have been rather precarious. At this point the person may need crisis intervention.

Such help is available from a number of agencies. Many communities have those who counsel people with acute problems. Suicide counseling, psychiatric emergency service, and centers with knowledge of community resources can be an invaluable help to those in trouble. They can support a person who is in a state of shock, directing him to professional help as well as plugging his problem into the proper resource to get clothes or a place to sleep; to get food or nursing service or hospital supplies. The Red Cross, Salvation Army, and local missions or other agencies can supply material help and also

---
* Lee, 1980

someone to listen when a person's life is disrupted by catastrophe.

These philanthropic organizations are not there primarily to offer therapy and make changes in the person as a human being. But many times the Lord uses these human support systems for help in the resolution of psychological crisis. Then, with the air cleared, the person may be able to continue his life through direct guidance by the Holy Spirit.

The Omniscience and Omnipotence of God

Finally, no one knows the mind of the Lord. The need for a personal relationship; the lack of introspection, or of psychological sophistication, or of discipline; the harmful practice of denial; the need for crisis intervention—these are some of the reasons why God directs His children into professional support systems as a framework for their growth. I say that He directs because, "The steps of a good man are ordered by the Lord" (Ps. 37:23). Of course there are other reasons which we may not have recognized here. Although I am not sure of all of these, I do have an answer for the person who demands, "Why is the Lord making me go through all this? Why doesn't He just deliver me out of my trial?" Unquestionably, the Lord can deliver us. But while He is a God of love and power, He is also a God of time and of purpose. Many times, I believe, He wants to deliver the believer through the situation, not from it. He wants us to exercise and to grow strong.

Only He knows the future. We should not try to place God in a box. Such attempts come from a desire to control situations because of a lack of trust. When we develop a scheme by which we expect God to work, we quench the Holy Spirit. God cannot be confined. He is not limited to the immediate or to the distant, to the natural or to the supernatural. But He knows what is best.

A chapter in Hebrews recounts some of the scores of lives which God changed and directed supernaturally;* but our Christian perspective is balanced by the remainder of this chapter on faith.** It describes other lives which followed a longer, more circuitous, more painful road in seeking "the promise" (Heb. 9:15; 11:39). We trust, hope, believe. God determines and decides.

We cannot help but see God's hand in everything concerning man, from his creation to his recreation. God knows about our conception. He programs our growth. He attends us when we are reborn. By His Spirit He nurtures our spiritual development, our psychological changes: He blesses our fruit-bearing. And by His grace He welcomes us at last to live and reign with Him forever.

---

* Heb. 11:1-35
** Heb. 11:36-40

REFERENCES

1. Altman, L.A. *The Dream in Psychoanalysis.* International Universities Press, 1969.
2. Baldwin, A.L. *Theories of Child Development.* John Wiley & Sons, 1968.
3. Balint, M. *The Basic Fault.* Tavistock Publications, 1968.
4. Billheimer, P. *Destined for the Throne.* Christian Literature Crusade, 1975.
5. Billheimer, P. *Don't Waste Your Sorrows.* Christian Literature Crusade, 1977.
6. Bowlby, J. *Attachment and Loss.* Attachment (Vol. 1), Basic Books, Inc. 1969.
7. Bridges, J. *The Pursuit of Holiness.* Navpress, 1978.
8. Cameron, N. *Personality Development and Psychopathology.* Houghton Mifflin, 1963.
9. Coleman, J.C. *Abnormal Psychology and Modern Life.* Scott, Foresman & Co., 1956.
10. Erikson, E.H. *Childhood and Society.* W.W. Norton, 1950.
11. Forer, L. *The Birth Order Factor.* David McKay Co., 1976.
12. Freud, S. *The Complete Introductory Lectures on Psychoanalysis.* W.W. Norton & Co., 1966.
13. Hall, C.S., and Lindzey, G. *Theories of Personality.* John Wiley & Sons, 1957.
14. Hollander, M. "Holding Patterns: Why Women Want More and Men Less." *Sexual Medicine Today, 4,* 1980, No. 8.
15. Kemper, T.D. "Mate Selection and Marital Satisfaction According to Sibling Type of Husband and Wife." *J. Marr. Fam.,* Aug. 1966, pp. 346-349.
16. LaHaye, T. *Spirit-Controlled Temperament.* Tyndale. House Publishers, 1966.
17. Lee, R.R. "He's Helping Ministers." In *Christian Herald,* Oct. 1980, p. 8.
18. Lewin, K. *Dynamic Theory of Personality.* McGraw-Hill, 1935.
19. Lovett, C.S. *Lovett's Lights on Romans.* Personal Christianity, 1976.
20. Menninger, K. *Whatever Became of Sin?* Hawthorn Books, 1973.
21. McDonald, R.L. *Memory Healing: God Renewing the Mind.* Crossroad Books, 1980.

22. McDonald, R.L. *Soul Prosperity.* RLM Ministries, Inc. (in press).
23. McDonald, R.L. *His Mind Within.* RLM Ministries, Inc. (in press).
24. Nee, W. *The Release of the Spirit.* Sure Foundation, 1965.
25. Noyes, A.P., and Kolb, L.C. *Modern Clinical Psychiatry.* W.B. Saunders Co., 1963.
26. Ovesey, L. *Homosexuality and Pseudo-Homosexuality.* Science House, 1969.
27. Packer, J.I. *Knowing God.* InterVarsity Press, 1973.
28. Parker, G.E. *Creation: the Facts of Life.* CLP Publishers, 1980.
29. Pink, A.W. *The Sovereignty of God.* Baker Book House, 1976.
30. Pink, A.W. *Practical Christianity.* Guardian Press, 1974.
31. Piaget, J. *The Construction of Reality in Children.* Basic Books, 1954.
32. Riggs, R.M. *The Spirit Himself.* Gospel Publishing House, 1949.
33. Roden, R. "Concept of Prenatal Affective Coding." *Current Concepts in Psychiatry,* 5, 1979, 2-11.
34. Schafer, R. *Aspects of Internalization.* International Universities Press, 1968.
35. Shafii, M. "Human Bonding and Child Development." *Current Concepts in Psychiatry,* 5, 1979, 12-14.
36. Shakespeare, W. *The Plays and Poems of William Shakespeare.* "As You Like It," The Outlook Co., 1899.
37. Spurgeon, C.H. "A Far-reaching promise." In *Metropolitan Tabernacle Pulpit,* Vol. 44. Pilgrim Publications, 1976.
38. Symonds, P.M. *The Ego and the Self.* Appleton-Century, Crofts, 1951.

"A Christian Psychiatrist Speaks Out"
on tape

RLM	1	The Role of Anger in the Life of the Believer
RLM	2	The Constructive Use of Anger
RLM	3	Depression: Cause and Treatment
RLM	4	Sickness and Healing
RLM	5	Knowing God, the Father
RLM	6	Mental Imges: Overcoming Made Easy
RLM	7	Guilt: What Kind Do You Have? (Part 1)
RLM	8	Guilt: What Kind Do You Have? (Part 2)
RLM	9	Afraid? Fear Not!
RLM	10	Memory Healing: God Renewing the Mind (Part 1)
RLM	11	Memory Healing: God Renewing the Mind (Part 2)
RLM	12	God's Perspective of Sex in Marriage
RLM	13	Emotions and Emotional Problems
RLM	14	The Human Spirit: What Is It?
RLM	15	Deliverance: Fact and Fantasy (Part 1)
RLM	16	Deliverance: Fact and Fantasy (Part 2)
RLM	17	Separation: It's Worth the Pain!
RLM	18	The Will and Spiritual Response Patterns
RLM	19	Identity: Basis for Christianity
RLM	20	Control: Who Needs It?
RLM	21	The Mind: Your Power or Satan's? (Part 1)
RLM	22	The Mind: Your Power or Satan's? (Part 2)
RLM	23	The Anatomy of Unforgiveness
RLM	24	Marriage: Uses and Abuses
RLM	25	Dreams: God's Night Messages
RLM	26	Your Fantasies Really Affect Your Life
RLM	27	In Search of Intimacy

Address all orders to:
RLM Ministries, Inc.
3390 Peachtree Road, N.E.
Atlanta, Georgia 30326
All tapes $3.50

EXPERIENCE HEALING NOW!

Read these other important books for spiritual growth, healing and wholeness.

Feeling and Healing Your Emotions by Conrad W. Baars, MD.
   A Christian psychiatrist shows you how to grow to emotional and spiritual wholeness.
P510-8
U.S. Price $5.95
Trade Paper

The Transformation of the Inner Man by John and Paula Sandford.
   The most comprehensive book on inner healing today: Beyond inner healing—complete transformation!
P539-3
U.S. Price $5.95
Trade Paper

Freedom From Depression by James E. Johnson.
   If you are one of the 40 million Americans who suffer from periods of depression, this self-help book will show you the causes, symptoms and treatment of depression.
P494-5
U.S. Price $2.95
Pocketsize.

ORDER TODAY!

**Bridge Publishing, Inc.
South Plainfield, NJ 07080**

248.4   HG369
M14

McDonald, Robert L.
THE HOW OF SPIRITUAL
GROWTH

31903010115422

BV4501.2 M135 / The how of spiritual growth